C000148462

CARNEGIE HALL
WITH TIN WALLS

CARNEGIE HALL
WITH TIN WALLS

FRED VOSS

BLOODAXE BOOKS

Copyright © Fred Voss 1988, 1991, 1992, 1994, 1995, 1997, 1998

ISBN: 1 85224 473 9

First published 1998 by
Bloodaxe Books Ltd,
P.O. Box 1SN,
Newcastle upon Tyne NE99 1SN.

Bloodaxe Books Ltd acknowledges
the financial assistance of Northern Arts.

LEGAL NOTICE

All rights reserved. No part of this book may be
reproduced, stored in a retrieval system, or
transmitted in any form, or by any means, electronic,
mechanical, photocopying, recording or otherwise,
without prior written permission from Bloodaxe Books Ltd.

Requests to publish work from this book
must be sent to Bloodaxe Books Ltd.

Fred Voss has asserted his right under
Section 77 of the Copyright, Designs and Patents Act 1988
to be identified as the author of this work.

Cover printing by J. Thomson Colour Printers Ltd, Glasgow.

Printed in Great Britain by
Cromwell Press Ltd

For my wonderful wife Joan

ACKNOWLEDGEMENTS

Acknowledgements are due to the editors of the following publications in which some of these poems first appeared: *Ambit, Bête Noire, Caprice, Chance, Lumpen, The North, One Dog Press, Pearl, Penniless Press, Poetry Review, Poetry Ireland Review, Prop, Royal Vagrant, The Rialto, Stand, Tears in the Fence, Wooden Head Review* and *The Wormwood Review.*

This edition includes 29 poems reprinted from *Goodstone* (Bloodaxe Books/ Event Horizon Press, 1991), which is now out-of-print, as well as poems first collected in the following pamphlets: *Goodstone Aircraft Company* (P.O. Press, 1988), *Memo #68* (Carnivorous Arpeggio, 1992), *Still in the Game* (BGS Press, 1994); *Maybe It's All True* (Pearl Editions, 1995), *The Sisyphean Burden* (Rose Bank Press, 1996); *Love Birds* (Chiron Review Press, 1997), *Butchers and Brain Surgeons* (Liquid Paper Press, 1997) and *Clear and Sharp* (Penniless Press, 1998).

CONTENTS

One of the Joys of the Job

Machinists
stick their chests out and shout, 'Yeah I'm an asshole!' or
'I'm a real ASSHOLE!' at each other.
They
rivet 'World Class Asshole' plaques onto the insides of their toolbox lids
and laugh
at each other whenever they can,
attaching rag and wire tails to each other's rear belt loops
and sneaking up behind each other to dribble water
out of squirt bottles down each other's legs
and dumping metal chips all over each other's toolboxes
and inviting each other outside
to fight.

Unlike all those people in offices,
machinists don't have to pretend
not to be assholes.

Inventive

The biker machinist
smoked non-filter cigarettes,
holding them between fingertips and thumb like they were joints
taking deep drags on them sucking them down to small stubs
which he then held
in a roach clip to take a few final hits
in front of a supervisor if possible.
The machinist on the milling machine with the computer
digital readout
smoked a pipe
as he spent hours and hours puzzling over the blueprints to
the parts to be made
as if he were a physics professor pondering Einstein's General
Theory of Relativity.
Wrongway
over on machine #470
smoked those big green cheap cigars,
tilted back in his leather swivel chair as his machine ran
automatically
and blowing huge lungfuls of smoke high up into the air
where they would drift
out over our machines in a 50-foot radius and descend
on us like a stinking fog
while he laughed until his fat belly bounced like a beach ball.

Machinists are far too colorful characters
to just smoke.

Keep Smiling

With the first storm of winter,
once again the Goodstone Aircraft Company machine shop roof
lets water pour through in columns
to collect in spreading puddles
all over the building,
and the machinists dust off the old jokes
about machine operators
wearing raincoats and standing under umbrellas
as they work,
nodding in familiar recognition as they look up at
a particularly big leak in the ceiling and saying,
'It rains harder in here than it does outside!'
or pointing at a rapidly spreading puddle
and saying,
'If that water reaches 440 volts, it'll be the highlight of somebody's day!'
as the Lead Man rides around on a bicycle
with a basket full of plastic sheeting
offering to sell it
to machinists
scurrying to cover up
electrical boxes and circuit breakers.

Choo! Choo!

Big Ed doesn't mind that the emolient
and the water
we mix to make coolant for our machines
are 100 yards apart
at opposite ends of the building separated
by our 3-rowed array of machinery,
he just stiffens his jaw
and takes hikes
with the 100-gallon steel barrel
on wheels,
pouring the quart of emolient into it at one end of the building
and then rolling the barrel
the length of the building toward the water faucet
at the other end,
digging into the concrete aisleway with his heels
and putting his muscle into it,
increasing the speed of the rolling barrel and getting a rhythm
going with the clacking of the wheels
over the bumps and cracks in the concrete aisleway,
able to keep control of the lurching directions of the barrel
so as to avoid running into
expeditors or supervisors walking the aisles
and yet able to increase the speed
of the clacking
to the point where the rolling barrel sounds just
like a train rolling down the tracks
and admiring machinists at their machines
are doing ear-splitting train whistle imitations
and lifting their caps and staring
with admiration.

Coping

After the 6:00 a.m. start-work buzzer
blares Mitch begins humming and la-laing
cha-cha rhythms louder and louder
as he fills out his time card at his workbench
until he turns toward Bobby
on machine #451 next to him and shouts, 'Suck my cock, BobBEEE!' in
cha-cha rhythm
cha-chaing his feet back and forth and beating out a rhythm
with his fists at his side as if he were holding maraccas,
turning around to face Alan
on machine #462 and sing out, 'Bend...over, AaaaLAN!' as he
grins and cha-chas his feet
then turns to face Tom across the aisle
at machine #456 and shout, 'Suck me off, TomMEEE!' and go
into a prolonged
near-hysterical giggle until he has to grab the edge of his
workbench to keep from falling over.

Some machinists
take having to be away from their wives 8 hours each day
pretty hard.

Improvizing

Machinists
use their airguns
which they have fitted with 3-foot-long aluminum
$1/4$ inch-in-diameter barrels
for many things
as their machines run,
they stick the tips of the barrels down
into round cutter holders or whatever weird
cavities they can find on the tooling
they are using or the parts they are cutting to imitate
whistles or horns blowing at shrill
shrieking decibel levels that have their fellow machinists
cringing and covering their ears and trembling with nerves,
and they fit
those halves of cardboard tubes the cutters come in
onto the tips of their airgun barrels and fire them
like missiles with deadly high-velocity and stinging accuracy
into each other's backs whenever
they can.

Only pussies
use those airguns strictly to blow the metal chips
off their machine tables.

Attacking the Problem

Goodstone Aircraft Company
attacks a problem by immediately
thinking of an acronym
such as
Quality Product Enhancement System, QPES;
or Part Conformity Assurance Program, PCAP;
or Parts Quality Team Management, PQTM.
Armed with the acronym,
they immediately make huge 100-foot-long
QPES or PCAP or PQTM
banners
and hang them across the tops of the walls of buildings
facing employee parking lots.
They immediately
print up thousands of posters
and tens of thousands of fliers and memos and bulletins
sporting the headline QPES or PCAP or PQTM,
handing them out at the plant gates
and pinning them to bulletin boards
in every building
as executives give speeches
and videocassettes are shown
expanding on the themes
of QPES or PCAP or PQTM.

Even though none of this
will actually affect the work being done on the shop floor,
it will give all of those people in the offices
something to do.

Disadvantage

The supervisor jabbers and screams
about how the machinist should do the job.
The supervisor throws parts around,
jams his fists into his pockets
and pumps himself up and down on the balls of his feet,
his face red
as he huffs and puffs.

But the machinist is calm,
listens politely and attentively to the supervisor,
waits for him to finish.

The machinist knows that the supervisor has a rough job,
having to somehow compensate
for the fact that he is supervising men
who for 20 years or more have run machines
that he has never run once
in his life.

The Standard of Excellence

The Air Force provides Goodstone Aircraft Company
with an S.A.P. AUDIT book.
The book tells the Goodstone Aircraft Company machinists
exactly which questions the Air Force's S.A.P. AUDIT
will ask and what the machinists' answers should be.
The book delineates all of the specifications and
regulations that the machinists have never abided by.
It tells the machinists exactly
how the shop should have been run
for the past 3 years,
so that the machinists can execute a crash
15-day cram session
on manufacturing orders and blueprints,
machine speed and feed calculations,
cleanliness and safety standards,
and tooling and material identification.

Our machinists will be proficient and efficient
and clean and safe.

What You Got for Your Tax Dollars

In the Goodstone Aircraft Company machine shop bathroom
at the end of each shift
we would butt elbows jockeying
to get to the sinks.
'Let a WORKING man through!'
inevitably brought raucous laughter, as did
'Boy, I really WORKED today!'
We would all smile and laugh and shake our heads
as we washed.
'How'd you get dirty, you fall off your stool?'
'People have been put in jail for stealing less money than
I do working here!'
'Yeah, I feel guilty when I stand in line to cash
my paycheck!'
Slapping and bumping each other in front of the mirror
with our $16-an-hour grins.
'Well, we fooled 'em again!'

One of the Great Secrets

The tool crib attendant
avidly
hands the air nozzle on the end of the compressed air hose
in his tool room to the veteran Lead Man
outside the gate who
once again tunes up by making 3 or 4 quick
squirts of air with the nozzle against the palm of his hand
producing random squeaks and whistles
then
lowers the nozzle to the jeans on his thigh
where with his special technique
developed over the years
he
with nozzle and fingers pressed against thigh jeans
makes a loud perfect
wolf whistle
of one ascending and then one descending
note,
once again
leaving the young tool crib attendant shaking his head
as he takes the air nozzle back
and makes futile attempts with it against a rag
making nothing but weak out-of-key
fart-like sounds,
leaving him with nothing to do
when that mouth-watering secretary walks by
but lean out over the gate
and run his hand rapidly up and down the gate post
like he was jacking off.

Lucky

I am machining
2 blocks of sawed aluminum bar stock
into 2 identical parts,
and filling out separate First Time Conformance cards
on each one
because each one came with its own separate
manufacturing order
bearing different part numbers, serial numbers,
and issue numbers,
and I am spending most of my time
confusing the 2 parts and then trying to re-identify them
and record
their different dimensions to the thousandth of an inch
in the tiny little boxes
all over the separate First Time Conformance cards,
and getting angry
over the fact that Goodstone Aircraft Company
didn't put the identical parts on one manufacturing order.

Of course, it could have been worse –
Goodstone could have followed its usual procedure
and sent me 1 part on 1 manufacturing order and then,
when I had finished the part and torn down
all of the complex set-ups and sent back
all of the special tooling and cutters
for the job,
sent me the second identical part on a separate
manufacturing order.

Righteous Indignation

Jack
worked at a snail's pace
throughout the shift when he wasn't
at the vending machines or some other machinist's
machine
bullshitting with other machinists for 15 or 30
minutes at a time.
Except when Goodstone Aircraft Company supervisors
said something to him about not accomplishing enough.
Then
he stomped around his machine fuming and saying,
'They PISSED me off!'
'They've PISSED me off NOW!' to any machinist who cared
to listen as
he proceeded to do absolutely nothing
for the rest of the day.

That would teach them
to insult someone with as much pride
as he had.

Who Cares?

A few months ago I was transferred to department PSLR
and I have since discovered that no one
in department PSLR knows
what PSLR means what the letters stand for I have been
all over the shop asking machinists what
the letters stand for and they all
shrug their shoulders and shake their heads
and say
they have no idea as if knowing the answer to that question
were the most meaningless, insignificant
and uninteresting thing in the world –
I guess
in a department where things make as much sense and inspire
as much enthusiasm
as they do in department PSLR,
it's just fitting
that no one knows.

Fan Club

Whenever Maintenance arrives
to work on one of our machines,
we make a point to gather about
the machine they are working on and stare at them,
munching apples and
leaning back with arms folded
elbowing each other in the ribs
as we crack jokes
at their expense,
chuckling and shaking our heads
and whistling the Oliver and Hardy theme
as the Maintenance men
sweat and strain and grapple,
turning and pushing and hammering
machine parts,
turning red with embarrassment
and cursing and having fits
because they know they must do a good job
if they don't want to endure
having us watch them all over again.

Therapy

Our machine shop supervisor
was always hiding behind posts
or hurrying up and down the aisles,
glancing about as if he was lost.
He began to stutter
and spend more and more time
in the toilet stalls,
until one day he climbed up onto one of our machines
and began screaming
that we were all against him.

We gathered about the machine he stood on
and looked up at him in silent respect
of his long-overdue decision
to deal with reality.

National Security

A man from the offices
comes by to lean over my toolbox and tell me in low voice
that the Air Force is coming through
and so the supervisor wants
the manufacturing orders and parts confomance charts
in their proper clear plastic folder-like
envelopes,
as he gathers the paperwork up from
my workbench and stuffs it all into the plastic envelope
so that I will have to take it out again
when I want to use it
later,
and sets the envelope down neatly onto the top of my toolbox
and walks off toward the next machinist.

It sure is good to know
that the Air Force is keeping a close watch
on such a really vital aspect
of our job.

Memo #68

My Lead Man
comes by with the Goodstone Aircraft Company memo
to all machinists consisting of a list of
largely indecipherable statistics regarding
management's goals for our performance as machinists
and our actual performance so far this year,
handing it to me along with a list of signatures.
'Here sign this paper here – that says that you promise
to read this memo and that you MIGHT understand it,' he
says, nodding his head as he goes into his smirking tongue-in-cheek
eyes-lifted-to-the-ceiling
look. 'Or at least that you might TRY to understand it!'
and I stick my tongue in my cheek and smirk
and roll my eyes and sign
and stuff the memo into my toolbox under a pile of wrenches
and files, knowing
that we'll have an equally indecipherable and forgettable
meeting
to explain the memo
anyway.

It's Okay

For years they'd seen
the KKKs drawn and carved in the bathroom stalls
and heard the nigger jokes,
but when they began to see hangman's nooses
hanging from the beams
above their machines,
the black machinists
began to get excited and angry demanding
an end as they screamed in white machinists' faces
things like 'Some of my relatives have died that way!' –
but Verl the old 39 year veteran
of the shop
didn't twitch a muscle or blink an eye
as he stayed stone-faced as ever
in the face of their screaming
and with utmost calm and reassurance
shrugged and said it was nothing it was just
that maybe the guys' sense of humor
went a little too far
sometimes.

The Aristocrats

The black machinists wore golden necklaces
and silky disco shirts
and dress pants
and Panama hats.
They bent and contorted their bodies over their machines,
twisting around grimy, oily
handles and spindles and fixtures
without once touching their clothes
to machine or tool or part.
They were constantly blowing every inch of their clothes
down with their air guns,
to make sure that not one metal chip or speck of dirt
spoiled their look.

26

Radios in their pockets and headphone wires to their ears,
they disco-danced up and down the wooden platforms
in front of their machines,
and disco-danced across the aisles
to each other's machines,
slapping hands and grinning,
triumphant.

Making the World's Most Advanced Bomber

The operators tried to make the machines
guide the half-ton bomber parts
into the razor-sharp cutters.

The old, worn-out machines rocked
as if they were about to tip over
under the weight of the bomber parts.
Gears ground and engines smoked
as the machines knocked and rattled inside,
starting and stopping without warning.

The foreman paced the aisles with terror in his eyes.

The operators avoided the machines.
They read newspapers in the bathroom,
shuffled back and forth from the vending machines,
and ran their fingers through piles
of old, stripped T-bolts

as they wondered what Goodstone Aircraft Company was doing
with the money
from its billion-dollar Air Force contract.

Hot Potato

We are supposed to cut weld preparations
along cracks in diffusion-bonded wing carry-thru sections
found piled outside Department 88,
so that welders can fill the cracks with titanium weld.

The Air Force wants the wing carry-thru sections NOW,
but we keep asking questions
about the unclear weld preparation blueprints.

Our foremen try to end our questions
by reading the blueprints upside-down
and giving us obviously bad advice.
They are beginning to avoid us
by hiding in the offices or walking laps
around the inside of the building.
When we press them, they refer us to supervisors
who shake their heads and refer us to manufacturing
engineers who shake their heads and carry the blueprints
into engineering offices which send the blueprints back
to us unchanged or even more unclear.

'JUST CUT IT!' the foremen scream at us.

We are beginning to feel uneasy.
We are beginning to wonder about those jokes
about the wings falling off the bombers.

For the first time in our careers, Goodstone Aircraft
Company has made us feel like responsible adults.
There must be something seriously wrong.

Solidarity

The workers
like to slam one heat-treated steel part against another
as they stack them in the steel bins.
After a worker executes a particularly loud ringing slam,
he will lift his face
to the tin ceiling 50 feet above
and begin hooting and screaming.
Other workers will join in
and the hooting and screaming
will grow louder and louder,
the workers encouraging and answering each other across the
steel mill
until every one of them is swept up
in a resounding chorus
that sends chills up the spines of the supervisors.

This is not the kind of cooperation
that the supervisors had in mind
when they talked to the workers
about working together for a better future.

Apprenticeship

The new man actually tried to work hard.

The veterans stared at him as if he were insane.
'Don't KILL the job!' they screamed.
They turned off his machine
and rolled his toolbox to the other end of the building.

The veterans were masters
at acting as if they were working.
They tapped parts
and studied indicators
and tightened and loosened and retightened bolts
hour after hour after hour,
accomplishing nothing.

Such consummate acting
was a skill that would take the new man years
to learn.

A Learning Experience

Every now and then
a new guy at Goodstone Aircraft Company
questions the way things are done.
Raising his hand at shop meetings
and writing letters to vice presidents
month after month after month,
he protests the inadequate tooling
and unclear blueprints,
expresses outrage
at the stacks and stacks of redundant paperwork,
bewails the lack of morale
and proper management,
and gets nowhere,
until finally he is reduced to lurching about the shop
blurting out truths and shouting incredulities
to machinist after machinist,
still getting nowhere,
and looking more and more each day
like that guy trying to stop cars on the highway
in *Invasion of the Body Snatchers*.

Cutting Corners

To position the half-ton wing carry-thru sections
on our machine tables,
our Lead Man
was always grabbing the 50-pound lead hammer
we refused to pick up
and holding it like a baseball bat swinging it
extra far back
digging his toes in throwing his entire body into it
and driving the head of the lead hammer
SMACK into the side of the titanium carry-thru section
that would join wings
and fuselage of a K-20 bomber,
as we remembered what we had been told
about never touching the sections
with lead hammers at all
because the lead contaminated the titanium
and caused cracks and imperfections
up to an inch beneath the surface
of the titanium.

Of course,
that was before
they'd found a big pile of fucked-up wing carry-thru
sections hidden in back of building 75
that had to be finished and delivered to the Air Force
right away.

Sometimes you can't afford
to be too picky.

Making America Strong

We worked nights as machine operators
at Goodstone Aircraft Company, where we made parts
for the Air Force's new bomber, the K-20.
In the parking lot, before work and during lunch break,
we drank and smoked dope and snorted chemicals.
At work we wore sunglasses
and danced in front of our machines.
We picked up bomber parts and blew through them
as if they were saxophones.
We stalked each other with squirt guns,
screaming and laughing and staggering.
We played with the overhead crane,
hoisting each other's tool boxes to the ceiling.
We unscrewed knobs from machine handles
and threw them around like baseballs.
Our foreman snuck drinks
from the bottle of vodka in his toolbox,
and paced about the shop in a daze.
We respected our foreman.
He'd given us some valuable advice.
'Whatever you do,' he'd warned us over and over, 'don't join
the Air Force and fly a K-20. It's gonna CRASH.'

Safety Net

On the horizontal mill in the back corner
we machined slots into the hinges
of escape hatches,
slots that would allow the escape hatches
to swing open
when Air Force crew members had to bail out
of crashing K-20 bombers.
With excruciating craftsmanship and care,
we used shimstock and C-clamps
and rubber mallets
to position the hatches,
taking days
to shave thousanths of inches
off the sides of slots
with saw cutters,
closing micrometers and running indicators
all over the surfaces of the slots
to make sure that they were as near to perfect
as possible.

We all knew
that if there were one K-20 bomber part
that would truly be indispensible to the preservation of
American lives,
it would be the escape hatch.

Critical Condition

The machinists were concerned –
Curly
hadn't been doing too well –
that from-behind pussy shot
of a woman bent over with her legs spread
that he moved along on the calendar on his toolbox
sticking it to the dates
when he had gotten laid by his wife,
hadn't moved in a long time and it was stuck way back
on the 11th and it was now
the 20th and his trademark grin
was becoming more and more forced as he tried to swagger about
and said 'I'm sorry'
whenever another machinist pointed out that his pussy shot
hadn't moved.

But the machinists really started to get worried
that morning of the 24th when they
passed by
his toolbox and saw
that he'd removed the pussy shot from his calendar
entirely.

A man who has lost his reason for being
is in real trouble.

The Immovable Object

Lincoln never accomplished anything.
He just walked around his machine all night
with his hands closed up into fists
sticking his chin out
defiantly
and talking back
to the foreman whenever the foreman told him to do anything,
until finally the foreman one day
standing atop the big inch-thick slab of steel
bolted to the table of Lincoln's milling machine
suddenly began shouting at the top of his lungs,

'You cocksucker Lincoln! You you cocksucker you don't do a
Goddamned thing I tell you you cocksucker you son of a bitch
every day I have to listen to you bitch and you never do a thing
I say you COCKSUCKER Lincoln EVERY day I have to hear you
bitch you cocksucker YOU COCKSUCKER LINCOLN – '

And 10 minutes later
Mitch went over to Lincoln
and asked him how it felt
and Lincoln shrugged cooly and said,
'He was just blowing off steam.'

When the Going Gets Tough

Whenever some machinist's cutter blows up or rips into a
part
screaming and tearing the part off the machine table
and bringing the machine spindle spinning at 1,000 or so rpm
to a slamming halt that sounds like a gunshot,
machinists all across the shop
let out with loud
wolf whistles of admiration
and screaming hoots of crazed delight
like a rodeo rider makes as the bronco he rides
breaks out of the gate,
and loud sustained applause,
leaving their machines
and slowly approaching the disaster in a closing circle
like fans
seeking out the star of a show,
as the machinist who had the accident trembles and stares
blinking
with shock at the jagged stub of a cutter
and the ruined part and torn up tooling,
doing his absolute best
to keep that smile
he has forced across his face.

Sleepworking

At Goodstone Aircraft Company,
the ultra-slow turning of the machine cutters
and dials
and the dropping of chips from the sliced metal surfaces
of bomber parts
becomes hypnotic,
and everywhere machinists are nodding,
mouths falling open, heads jerking back,
as they snort and snore.

But over the years they have learned
how to keep themselves propped up
against the leather of their swivel chairs
without falling out of them,
and somehow
they are able to wake up just as their machines' cuts
are ending. They walk to the drinking fountain
and sprinkle ice-cold water on their heads,
or stand before fans
lifting their T-shirts up to their armpits,
knowing just how much to wake themselves up
so that they can reset their machines
for the next cuts.
Then they wiggle their asses
back into the impressions they have carved into
the leather of their chairs,
and get some more sleep.

Tool of the Trade

The machinists used their rollaway toolboxes like billboards,
plastering them with stickers and photos and posters
advertising their families,
their hobbies,
their opinions.
They filled them with booze and cigars and girlie magazines.
Parking them between their machines and the office,
they hid from supervisors
behind them.
Placards on their lids
threatened anyone who touched the rollaways
with death.

These machinists took their work seriously.

Excretion

The workers
cover the bathroom stall walls
with messages
calling each other rat finks
who suck the cock
or lick the ass
of the boss.
They call each other faggots and niggers and kikes
and Buddaheads and donkeys.
They use knifetips to carve
KKKs and swastikas
and 'Kill the Jews' into the wood of the stalls,
leaving unsigned threats about meeting each other
outside the plant gate–
while out on the shop floor
they smile at each other
and work together
cheerfully,
fully relieved by their stints
in the bathroom.

A Company Fence

Along the tunnel
that leads from the gate of Goodstone Aircraft Company down
under the boulevard and up to the employee parking lot across
the street,
3 x 5-foot sheets of formica
have been wire-bound along the chain link fence
that separates the workers' walkway
from the one-lane roadway that runs through the tunnel.
The formica sheets
do not lessen the nerve-shattering impact
of the towmotors and forklifts
running in low gear up the grades of the tunnel,
nor do they keep out the dizzying, nauseating exhaust fumes,
but they do give the workers the opportunity
to bang their swinging fists against them
as they march by
going home from work
in a 100-foot-long single-file line.
Everywhere up and down the line, the fists of laughing machinists
suddenly slam like sledgehammers
into the center of the formica sheets,
making them crack and boom and echo in the tunnel
as though cranked up by amplifiers
next to the machinists' ears,
and all up and down the line
the raw-nerved machinists
are cringing and pulling their heads down toward their shoulders
and exploding
into uncontrollable jerks and spasms
as they fall victim to each other's
calculated pauses
and sudden, unexpected cracks and booms.

They are making the most of this one last chance
to fuck with each other's
nervous systems
as they leave their screaming machines behind.

Advantage

The medication
the graveyard shift machinist took left him unperturbed
and cool as a cucumber no matter what
the supervisors or the manager said to him no matter how
loudly or abusively they insulted or threatened him no matter what
impossibly difficult jobs they gave him and no matter how soon
they wanted the jobs done no matter how angry
other machinists got at the terrible
inept and dangerous setups he left them on their machines
no matter how much
they screamed and threw clamps and bolts and stools around.
It always kept him absolutely unruffled
and indifferent.

That medication may have kept him from having a nervous breakdown
but it was about to give one
to everyone he worked with.

Graphic Demonstration

Whenever
Curly picked up a can of blue Dykem layout dye
to spraypaint a part before etching layout lines onto it
he would shake the can up
and lower it to his fly and spray a big streak of blue
like it was coming out of his cock and whenever
enough machinists were watching
Curly would pick up his spray bottle of coolant
and spray a long stream
from crotch level but his favorite
was that 9-inch-tall bottle of white paste
that he would stick out from his fly and stroke
and then squeeze out
a long milky stream of paste that arched
10 feet to splat
against a cabinet face or a workbench
or a machinist.

Just telling his fellow machinists over and over
that he was separated from his wife
and wasn't getting enough.

Go with the Flow

The Goodstone Manufacturing Standards
books are in 5 volumes that are each 4 inches thick
and 12-inches-high
and stacked
at several strategic locations around the machine shop,
full of standards for things like
finish and squareness and taper and concentricity
tolerances
on the aircraft parts we manufacture,
but only once
in the 2 years I have worked at Goodstone Aircraft Company
have I actually seen someone
drag one of the 10-pound volumes off a shelf
and carry it to their workbench and thumb through it
looking to see if the part they were making
was within Goodstone Manufacturing Standards' tolerances,
even though every blueprint we use
states that we are to work according to
those standards.

After all of those hundreds and hundreds of aircraft
we've made,
I guess none of us wants to be the one
to discover
what we might have been doing wrong.

Not Amused

Curly
sat by himself way in back of the conference room
with a 3-day growth of beard and a grimy unwashed face
and a month's worth of being without his wife who
had left him,
glaring at the manager
who had just given his usual talk to the machinists about
how he wanted the machinists to tell him what they thought
was wrong with the machine shop so that he
could correct it,
and when the manager asked if there were any suggestions

Curly raised his hand and said, 'You know,
this is just the same old SHIT, you get up there and say
you're gonna do something, how we're gonna get the tooling
and the cutters we need and stuff,
and then nothing gets DONE, it's all a bunch of
FUCKING SHIT that we've all heard a dozen times before and
it's a GODDAMN SHAME and it MAKES ME WANNA PUKE,
all this BULLSHIT about doing things that we all know
are never gonna get done, it's all the same old SHIT
and it's just gonna make us all DISGUSTED and
PISSED OFF and not give a FUCK!!'

Curly
just isn't quite his usual perpetually smiling congenial
self when he isn't getting laid.

Honkers

The workers
make the most of the echo chamber
acoustics of the tin
50-foot-high building
to showcase
their sneezes –
one does a kind of
screaming birdcall,
another a bronco-busting
rodeo star 'YaaaHOOO!'
as he rears his head back
then throws it down
to jump back with the explosion.

But the forklift driver
has them all beat,
driving around
sounding his horn
with his right hand
just as he buries his nose
into the handkerchief
in his left.

Playground

Machinists
hook wire and cloth tails
to the belt loops on the backs of each other's pants or
glue nude photos of hairy cocks and balls on top of
each other's ID photos or pin
company newspaper photos of each other onto the main aisle bulletin
board with written-in captions like 'Gay Machinist of the Month'
or roll big rolls of masking tape up and down the aisles at each other
like bowling balls or make those super
rockets
out of cardboard cutter tubes and tape and modelling clay
that they fire
off their 105-pounds-of-air-pressure airgun tube nozzles
high up into the air and hundreds of feet across the machine shop
where they land on machinists or hit
the tin machine shop wall 50 or 60 feet above the floor
and hopefully stick,
the machinists going into hysteria laughing and grinning and
leering with the joyful juvenile delinquent excitement of someone
who has just set off a cherry bomb during the school assembly.

Not many 30 or 40 or 60-year-olds
can get paid
to be 9 years old.

Bubbling Over

He couldn't stop
slipping those big pistol-like parts through his belt
and walking around pulling them out
pretending to fire them at machinists,
or walking around with long aircraft spar parts
in his hands, opening and closing their opposed ends
like the jaws of an alligator
as he worked his own jaws up and down
making weird grunts.
He couldn't stop
going up to some machinist
with a long cylindrical part
and blowing through the part as if he were
doing a trumpet call,
then loudly announcing the machinist's name
as if he were announcing a king.
He just couldn't stop putting
a big C-clamp around his head
and closing its steel pads against his temples
and walking up to machinists telling them
how he had this pressing pain in his head
and asking them for aspirins.

Being a machinist at his machine
just wasn't good enough for him.

The Mantra

At 7:00 a.m.
unlocking his toolbox and throwing open its lid he'll begin
yelling, 'Fuck. Fuck. Fuck.' And then
looking over at me with wild-eyed
despair say,
'Fuck it Fred!' Fuck it Fred! Fuck it Fred!'
waiting for me to look and then
slamming his airgun down onto his sheet-metal workbench top
so that it SLAPS and yelling,
'Fuck this place! Fuck this place!'
waiting for me to nod and then taking out his hammer
and pounding out an ear and nerve shattering drum roll
against a particularly reverberative steel section of his
machine,
turning to stare at me with legs spread, shouting out as
loud as he can, 'Fuck 'em! FUCK 'EM ALL, FRED! FUCK 'EM
ALL IN THE ASS!!'

It's just a little early morning
Goodstone Aircraft Company ritual he goes through
that makes him feel better.

The Criminologist

After hearing
all of Curly's stories
about those Mexicans down on the computer mills talking
about how I look and act just like a mass murderer
and after hearing all of Curly's theories and insights
concerning why
my quiet undercover never-speaking super-nice-guy
manner
qualifies me as a possible PSYCHO who may
snap at any moment who may
attack someone with a wrench who may
have 17 people buried in his basement,

44

Earl
comes over to my machine to repeat Curly's allegations to me
and get my reaction to them
and I tell him
that he needn't worry that the only person
I might ever actually kill
would be Curly.

No Doubt

Our Lead Man
smiled at the idea
that some people said
we machinists at Goodstone Aircraft Company wasted a great deal
of money
for no reason by taking so ridiculously long
to produce K-20 Bomber parts.
Whenever the issue was brought up by any machinist,
our Lead Man
would just lean back and lift his chin in the air and fold
his arms across his chest
and get that super-confident twinkle in his eye
and smile on his face as he looked down at the machinist and
said, 'It's been PROVED that if you go any faster you make MISTAKES.
It's been proved that you can't go no faster than this!
It's been proved by a SCIENTIFIC STUDY!'

Undoubtedly,
that study was conducted
by Goodstone Aircraft Company.

Thin Line

Every few days
the K-20 Bomber production manager
grabs the Drill Press Lead Man from behind
and pulls him back in his swivel chair
choking his neck
and grinning/grimacing
with fun/murderous intent,
the Lead Man swiveling and the manager choking
until the Lead Man is pulled out of the chair
and he and the manager are wrestling across the machine shop floor,
rolling in the paperwork that spills
out of the expeditors' bicycles
they knock over,
as they call each other sons of bitches –
everyone running machines
or climbing stairways
or sitting at desks
around them
stopping to stare and listen waiting
to either laugh or rush in to prevent a murder,
knowing that the Lead Man and the manager
are no more sure than anyone else
whether they are joking or not.

No George Washington

Curly holds out a time-card the supervisor gave him
and now he's doing a celebration dance
like a touchdown scorer in the end-zone,
flopping about the huge mop of Afro-like curls on his head
and saying to me,
'You know, Fred, Goodstone's TESTING me, they say I forgot
to fill out my timecard last Thursday – the Thursday I wasn't here,
remember? – and Ron says for me to fill out this time-card
so I can correct my mistake of not turning in a card and get PAID
for last Thursday...,' Curly, giggling as his uncontrollably
delighted smile begins to make his eyes water, saying, 'You know,
Fred, Goodstone's testing my MORAL FIBER...

46

they're testing my INTEGRITY...'
Curly dance-stepping about
knowing that I know as well as he
that Goodstone
couldn't have made a more totally misguided
strategic error.

More Than Enough

'You're gonna miss me, Fred!!' Curly shouts
back at me as he rolls
his toolbox and cabinet
away from the machine next to me down toward
machine #620 50 feet away,
but since
for the last 6 months I have heard nothing but every detail
of Curly's private life and his reading to me
of Ann Landers' columns and comic strips and
his imitations of Conan O'Brien and
Seinfield and *The Simpsons* and Pee
Wee Herman and his repeating to me
of the remarks of radio talk-show hosts and callers
he listens to on his headphone radio
as well as his descriptions
of his shits in the bathroom and of how far his cum spurted
when he jacked off the other night,
I doubt it.

Reprieve

When the final buzzer sounds
throughout building 8,
machinists jump to life
for the first time that day,
bustling in a line
to the final punching of the timeclock
to charge out the door,
legs and arms pumping and eyes brightening
as they get their circulation and alertness back
and regain full lung capacity,
breathing huge sighs of relief
as they increase speed
heading toward the guard gate
and laugh, pointing at the speed and energy of those ahead of them
saying things like 'What drive!'
or 'What initiative!'
and making jokes
about the resurrection of the dead.

Down But Not Out

Maybe the greatest thing about our Sunday pickup softball game
was that
no matter how lonely
or poor
or hungover or strung out or
fresh out of a mental hospital
or jail or
hated by our parents or
stuck-on-a-nowhere-job-that-was-breaking-our-spirit-and-mind
any of us were or
no matter how ugly and small and cockroach-infested of an apartment
we lived in or
how many times we may have tried to kill ourselves,
any one of us might still
step up to the plate
and hit a home run.

Anyone
who can hit a home run
still has a chance
to turn their life around.

On Stage

Little Bob
came from back East on vacation to visit
his brother Bob the second baseman Little Bob
kept a huge muffler around his neck hanging
to his knees as he stepped
up to the plate and everyone in the field
hollered and screamed for him to assume
a batting stance as he kept showing
the fielders his profile with his nose up in the air
like he was a rock star and they were a crowd
screaming for an encore and when he finally
did pick up the bat and square up
at our car-mat home plate like he was going to hit
he only took one practice swing
and then stepped back before the pitcher could toss the softball
and turned the end of the bat toward his face
to grab it with both hands
and stick it to his mouth and scream Rod Stewart's
'Do Ya Think I'm Sexy?' into it
as if it were a microphone.

A few minutes later our relief
at his finally batting and hitting the ball
was short-lived
as we soon found out that he intended to sing
at every base he reached and stood on
too.

Competitive Spirit

The biker may have
looked awkward at the plate swinging wild golf swings
that missed the softball by a foot most times leaving
him collapsed in the dirt around the car mat
we used for home plate but when
he did connect his wild arms and legs that
moved in crazy flailing motions as he ran
came in handy as he made the most of his crazy self-destructive
reputation by barreling down the line
toward first base like he'd charge right into the first baseman
and he did
if the first baseman didn't get off the base he
flew flailing into him with cowboy boots kicking
and fists whirling like a windmill in front of his face
as he flattened the first baseman and then
crawled scrambled and/or ran
over him yelling those high-pitched giggling half-yodelling
screams that he screamed when he was really happy
turning the corner and heading down toward second where the
second baseman had to decide whether this was just a game in which
he could afford to step aside
or if he thought the possibility of getting the biker out
was important enough to stand on the base and get into a fistfight
or maybe even a knifefight over.

That biker couldn't hit
but he sure made the most of what he could do.

Still in the Game

Captain Tom was small and pale
and bone-thin tattooed and shaky with
jailhouse and mental hospital damage and he
stepped up to our car-mat home plate
in the dirt under the tree with a grinning
giggling kind of apologetic humor blinking behind his
coke bottle lenses as he swung and swung
and missed and missed over and over and over
in our can't-strike-out
take-as-many-swings-as-you-need-to-hit-the-ball
pick-up softball game as we
in the field took the opportunity to reach down
and lift our beer cans off the grass to our mouths
and take long relaxed drinks
and his teammates at bat said nothing
as he took up to 5 minutes to hit the ball and then
was almost invariably thrown out –
we all knew
that Captain Tom was accomplishing a major achievement
just stepping up to the plate.

Technique

When Mary
came to the plate she laughed bending over
in her tight TIGHT shorts to grab dirt
and dust the handle of the bat with it she giggled and panted
lasciviously as she propped herself
against the bat's ball-end handle that was jammed into
her crotch,
the end of the bat in the dirt by home plate
as she wobbled and rotated her hips
on the handle stretching her arms and fingers and then
sticking her ass out in the air taking
golf-swing-like girlish hopelessly ineffective chops
at the slow-pitched softball swinging and missing until
she'd dribble a grounder to the pitcher or an infielder
and she was off running swinging
her raised arms from side to side making
her huge tits sway and bounce
as much as possible while she ran
and though she almost never
made it to first base safely,
she did have every biker and other man at the game
trying to get in her pants
after it was over.

Aircraft Factory Love

The nude dance bars
on the streetcorners were always there
just down the street from Goodstone Aircraft Company.
Machinists
passed them on the way to work
and on the way home from work
with all that $22-an-hour 50-hour-a-week money
in their wallets,
and the loneliest machinists
spent all their free time in them
and fell in love with the strippers,
with women who ate fire
and belonged to nudist clubs
and pulled out leather whips
and practiced witchcraft,
the loneliest ones
gave them money
and moved in with them and were taken
for the rest of their money
and dumped,
ending up
with broken hearts they couldn't hide telling everyone
at work how much they loved those women,
trying to kill themselves
and hanging by threads
under psychiatric care,
shells of men
on machines
spending all their free time in nude dance bars
and saving their money again
for the next
love of their life.

Don't Call Me Shakespeare

All I had
for a woman were pictures in pussy magazines,
but I had
those 20-foot steel bars I shoved into and out of blast furnaces
across roller bars I had
the cutting torch that blasted blue oxygen
that could cut my hand off and
3-foot-long steel tongs to stack
the red-hot steel shanks I cut out of the bars I had
an English literature Ph.D. I'd flushed down the toilet with the
puke of a hundred hangovers I had
all the books I'd sold for beer money
and the stink of burning steel and gas stinging my nostrils
and swaggering hard hatted steel mill buddies
who talked about nothing
but pro sports and County Jail and pussy
and thought Shakespeare was a faggot,
to make me a man.

Self Preservation

The pussy men
buried their faces in the pages
of pussy magazines.
They had pussy shots on their keychains
and the insides of their toolbox lids.
They talked about pussy constantly,
about all of the pussy they had fucked,
and all of the ways they had fucked it.

The gun men
puffed on long cigars
and read gun magazines.
They wore gunshop T-shirts
and covered their toolboxes
with gun photos and NRA stickers.

They marched around their work areas
keeping their machines spotless by blasting them with
air guns they had fitted with 3-foot-long barrels.

No one survived
in that machine shop
without guns or pussy.

Rough Job

The machinist who tried to kill himself
because he couldn't stop crying like a girl
when he was on PCP;
the machinist holding up the pussy magazine
in front of his face
to be sure everyone knows he's staring at it;
the machinist in a constant rage
because his wife won't give him a blowjob;
the machinist telling everyone how much he hates
the queers on the 2nd tier of the L.A. County Jail;
the machinist who walks around with a tape measure
pulled out to 12 or 15 inches
and held in front of his fly;
the machinist who wears a hat saying 'U.S. Male'
and smokes big cigars
and weightlifts steel bars and arbors
while his machine runs:

being a man in a machine shop
is not easy.

8 Hours at Goodstone Aircraft Company

An hour to find a Hartford chuck,
half an hour to find a key for the Hartford chuck,
half an hour hammering on the chuck
because its rotation turns out to be jammed,
half an hour cursing Goodstone Aircraft Company,
an hour walking through 2 buildings
looking for another Hartford chuck,
an hour in a bathroom reading a sports page
to keep from going berserk,
another half an hour looking for a chuck.
An hour looking for 2 bolts
to lock the chuck you have finally found
onto your milling machine table.
15 minutes of throwing tools around,
kicking cabinets
and yelling obscenities
after you discover that the jaws will not close on the chuck
that you have bolted onto your milling machine table.
The remaining hour and 15 minutes spent
shuffling about 3 buildings
in a pretense of looking for another chuck
that you know you will never find,
that you no longer WANT to find,
that you no longer have the morale or energy
to do anything with
anyway.

A Threat

My fellow workers and I
operate machines that cut steel blocks.

As the machines cut the steel,
my fellow workers like to stare and laugh at each other.
They are ready to piss on each other's graves.

They fear me.
They call me crazy.
They don't like the poetry I read.
They don't like the paintings I have hung
on the board behind my machine.
They look at me
like they want to cut my balls off.

Tomorrow I think I will start bringing roses to work.
Each day I will stand a rose in a jar of water
on the workbench behind my machine.
I want to really terrify my fellow workers
this time.

The Stud

He had worked out at Gold's Gym
until he could bench-press 450 pounds.

He walked around the machine shop
waving a 50-pound lead hammer above his head
with one hand,
and his hammer blows
echoed off the machine shop walls
like gunshots.

Then he started talking
about how much he liked to fuck
his boyfriend.

For the first time in the machine shop's 20-year history,
no one was telling any faggot jokes.

The Inspection

Whenever a good-looking secretary walks down the aisle at
Goodstone Aircraft Company,
the machinists make a point of staring at her
from the moment they spot her.
They move around their machines
to keep her tits and ass and thighs
in view,
making sure that it is obvious
they are watching her.
They drift away from their machines,
sticking their necks out into the aisle
to keep her in view
until she is out the door of the building.
Then they let out with shrill whistles,
shaking their heads and hands
and going limp all over as if they were about to collapse,
making sure that everyone knows
how much their lustful minds sucked in
every inch of every curve on her body,
competing with each other
to see who
can stagger and whistle and maintain
their open-mouthed blank-eyed look
the longest,
glancing about at each other
to take stock of the results.
Finally, when it is safe to quit whistling and moaning
tributes to her body,
they return to their machines,
reassured that they have once again passed
the test.

Lifesavers

Just
a clickclack of a secretary's highheels
across the concrete factory floor just
a scent of her perfume in the steel dust air just
a memory of the way his mother
touched him the last time he saw her or the beautiful checkout lady
at the supermarket smiles at him just
a memory of the way his last lover held his cock
in her mouth so long ago or
a green tattoo of a naked lady dancing
on his arm as he turns a machine handle or the flesh
of that beautiful young girl in that picture on the side
of his toolbox
drawn gratefully into the embrace of the soul
of a machinist who must work
the rest of his life away inside the tin walls of shops
full of nothing but the hardness
of men,
may be enough to make the difference between life
and death.

Soft Spot

Our old Lead Man walks the machine shop
with green tattoos of naked women
all over his biceps and a jaw
that he keeps clenched
like he just might
strike out at somebody at any moment with his fists for saying just
one wrong word to him or giving him one wrong glance or maybe
just because he feels like it just because
he's a mean tough bastard
to the bone though
we machinists all know that it's really clenched
to keep back the tears
for his wife
dead just 6 months.

Standout

The beautiful girl at the pipe-bending machine
lifts pipes
out of the bin to her right then sticks them into the machine that bends them
       then
drops them into the bin to her left all day with her
beautiful shiny long hair tied up in a bun
on top of her head she
swings her breasts
and rotates her hips stuck out into the dank
stinking-with-fumes-and-steel-dust air
as she swivels
her hourglass figure and smiles surrounded
by all the sweating strutting men at the other machines,
smiles
radiantly, shining more beautifully
here than any other beauty in the world
in her greasy blue denim apron
and black steel-toed boots.

Cold Nights

We
young steelworkers thrown out of homes
onto our own without mothers without
wives without women worked
at the steel mill every night until midnight next
to those roaring
white-hot blast furnaces that licked
at our forearms and faces and singed the hair off of them
as we rolled the 20-foot bars of steel in and out of them,
we hugged
close to those furnaces' fiery heat that meant money
in our pockets and food and beer in our bellies,
hugged close
in our steel-toed boots and gloves and hardhats and face shields
grateful
for the only warmth
in our lives.

The Gesture

Tim
spent his entire half-hour lunch breaks
perched on his stool over pieces of paper on top
of his rollaway toolbox writing
letters
to an old girlfriend who lived 3,000 miles away
in New York,
practically weeping as he bent over them writing,
telling
any machinist who would come by and listen
how much he loved her even though he hadn't even kissed her
once in their 5-year relationship,
how much he loved her and how futile it was how cursed
he was with women they just didn't like him
he didn't have what they wanted
he'd TRIED so hard for so long and he just didn't know
if he could take the heartache anymore,
then putting his trembling pen to paper once more
and forcing it to write to her
as if it were torturing him.

At least all of those machinists who were calling him
a faggot
couldn't say he hadn't tried.

Real Life

Surrounded by the steel cutting tools
and bars and arbors and the cold concrete floor
covered with metal chips and the oil and the 10-ton
rolling overhead cranes, my fellow machinists
shout and swing their arms
to pound and lock and measure,
and read nothing but race results or porno mags or motorcycle mags
and laugh and swear and act as much like children or beasts
as they can,
while at lunchbreaks I read Melville or Flaubert or Dostoyevsky
to make my spirit, my eye,
my heart
as strong and real and beautiful
as my fellow machinists.

Open Books

Sitting at the formica tables lined up on the concrete floor
in building 147 at lunch we workers
shovel slices of Christmas pizza bought for us by Goodstone Aircraft Company
into our mouths as hundreds of flood lights
shining from the ceiling 50 feet above beam down and reflect
back off the shiny yellow formica tabletops and
light up our faces
in cruel glare,
so that it seems as if for the first time I am seeing
those faces,
faces slashed with lines in brutal
patterns in all directions,
with smile lines
frown lines the lines of worry all over a black man's
face the lines
of alcoholism of 3-packs-a-day-smoking of
wild laughter and terror and lust and all the kinds of hard living
that must be lived to make it through
10 or 20 or 40 years of working in a factory building,

faces
that no executive or company president in an office
could have faces
that have the insides and the souls of these workers
written all over them and are more beautiful
because of it.

Success

I dropped out
of the U.C.L.A. Ph.D. program in English literature
to fill up a box each night with Schlitz cans
in a boarding house,
wearing a Greek fisherman's cap I found in the street
and playing harmonica to blues
that I blasted full volume
out of my 1957 stereo.
Big black Japanese cockroaches
made the Schlitz cans in the box in the corner of my room
tinkle
as I slept and woke and slept and woke
in my sweaty drunken stupors
all night
and rose in the morning to wash pots and pans across the street
in the dorm
with the black man who was dying
and constantly pouring vodka into orange juices
as he worked.
It was the best time of my life,
all those students carrying textbooks
up the hill
as I sold mine
for beer money,
and knew that the whole real world waited ahead
for me.

Green Thumb

I had to
retreat into a life without writing
or feeling, back into
an old cheap apartment where I hid for years
driving up and down Anaheim Street to work an unskilled job
and do nothing
but drink and jack off and nearly kill myself
in accidents with mattresses and ovens,
in the reek of alcohol and tabacco and dust and vomit to waste
away waiting
on emptiness inside the blank apartment walls with no reason
to live,
for the poem
to arrive, the
first poem that I had absolutely no control over
the poem that wrote itself
the poem that needed a soil
full of death
to grow out of.

Alchemy

Art can be made out of
the beautiful girl
who took every ounce of love in my heart away with her
and laughed at me as she opened her legs
to the first man she met in the bar art can be made out of
having nothing
left to go on with but the desire
to go on out of
empty dresser drawers and blank walls and days
so long they seemed like Hell and tears
after 15 beers at 2 a.m. for the 100th time
listening to Hank Williams's 'I Can't Help It If I'm Still in Love with You'
and the cold sheets
of pussy magazines and old dying alcoholic neighbors on Relief
who all thought I was crazy and a 5-year-old Doors concert ticket

from that one month I was with that beautiful girl and
an oven and the gas waiting for me to stick my head inside as I spent nights
on my knees peeking through corners of a curtain hoping
for the girl in the apartment behind to undress art
can be made out of all of this and I don't think
I would be alive today
if it couldn't.

All the Way

If I was going to write about working I wanted
to put on
steel-toed boots and uniforms with my name
above the left pockets and go to work
in factories and machine shops for good,
I didn't want
just a summer or a year or 2 I
wanted a permanent address in some neighborhood
full of pipefitters with those hats covered with crazy patchworks of
colors and
graveyard shift janitors and aging waitresses
with faces crosshatched by lines from the strain of decades of racing
all over coffee shop floors and Mexican
busboys or punch press operators living 3
or 4 to an apartment and steel mill
veterans with bellies huge and hard with beer and muscle I wanted
to know
that for the rest of my life I would be carrying lunch pails
down streets to my car
with them to drive my life away to and from
jobs I wanted my life
to be my art.

Each Machinist Is Different

A machinist
might do many things with the chips of aluminum or steel
or titanium that fly or fall off
of a cutter as it cuts a part on his machine,
if he has nothing to do he
might sweep them into a pile on the floor and push the pile
around and around his machine with a pushbroom
to look busy or
if he is bored
as his machine runs through one long droning automatic cut
after another
he might push them into a mound
on his mill table and sculpt them
into weird forms then spray paint them in psychedelic
wavy rings of purple and lavender and red layout dye,
or if he's mad at some night shift man
on his machine he might sweep up a shovel-full
of particularly stinky soaked-in-fetid-machine-oil
chips and dump them
all over the offender's toolbox, or
if he's a real 'Psychoman' like Ed was
and mad at everybody
get a nice dust-pan full of tiny aluminum chips
and dump them
into that big 10-gallon coffee maker
the machinists
drink from.

Capital Crime

He was a big muscular
biker with a booming voice who swaggered and was constantly
worried about his rollaway toolbox he would come in
at the beginning of his night shift each afternoon
to inspect
his rollaway toolbox thoroughly up and down on all sides
and check its position from different angles
and immediately
if he found that his rollaway toolbox had been moved
by a fraction of an inch or that a mark
down to the most microscopic barely visible
nick
had been made on it
he would begin the most frantic relentless
and indignant interrogation of dayshift machinists all around
the area
to try to determine
who the culprit was
as if it was a matter of life and death.

After all,
a whole lot of big bellowing swaggering and commanding
manhood
depended on it.

Sun Worshipper

It always made me feel better
to see the sunlight
as I worked in the steel mill,
I'd look up at the plastic windows in the 100-foot-high wall
to see it
whenever I could as I
stood on the cold concrete floor and gripped the cold
blocks of steel and machine handles and I'd
feel especially good
when a shaft of that sunlight pointed
down through a high window
to strike the concrete floor or
my machine I'd stand in the shaft of light
it was
magic on my skin
and I'd walk out on the asphalt
along the tin wall outside the steel mill
to stand in the sunlight and stare at it burning
on the asphalt all around my shadow until I believed
that I wasn't my shadow at all
but rather the sunlight
all around it.

Crossing Fingers

My Lead Man
is trying to get the aircraft part Manufacturing Orders and
the blocks of material the aircraft parts
are to be made out of,
together.
They had been together in the box on the rack
by my machine yesterday but overnight they got separated
and he finally locates the block of material
that LOOKS just like the right one
down at the other end of the building with no
manufacturing order along with a manufacturing order
that SHOULD fit the block of material
sitting in the box by my machine,
and he comes back from the other end of the building to throw
the block of material and the manufacturing order back
into the box
on the rack by my machine saying, 'Now we've got it straightened
out – at least, I HOPE so!' and walking off.

I hope so too,
especially when I think of the words of that supervisor
who had gone out of his way to tell us how
making a part out of the wrong piece of material
could cause 300 deaths
in a plane crash.

Dangerous

In the steel mill I never talked
to the machinists who worked on the machines around me
making them
suspicious and uncomfortable making them
stare at me out of the corners of their eyes as they turned
the handles to their machines
making them aim
the hot sharp steel chips that flew off their cutters
at me
to see what I'd do making them
come over and walk around my machine and stare up at me and
say, 'Don't step inside my aura!',
they were always glancing at me
as if I might blow up any minute as if I might
suddenly grab a 40-pound steel wrench
and start beating them over the head with it.

No.
I just wanted to write some poems
about them.

Something None of Us Ever Talked About

For five minutes or so some mornings
as we stood on the cold concrete steel mill floor
at 6:55 or 6:58 am
and drank black coffee,
all the machines
and the crane chains so absolutely still
and the furnaces so cold
would seem so quiet
we could almost hear our hearts pounding,
so quiet
we might almost have begun really talking to each other
for the first time,
so quiet
we might even have begun to tell each other
our dreams,
until
that screaming ear-shattering 7:00 am whistle
set our hundred pairs of hands to pushing Machine Start buttons
and firing up furnaces
and grabbing crane control boxes
and pulling and throwing machine handles and levers
and the roaring burning slamming pounding quaking non-stop turning
of steel into parts
made sure we would never have to know each other at all.

Clean

Every Friday afternoon
after stripping off my blackened grease-splattered shirt and pants
and taking a shower washing off the coolant and the cutting oils
and the black machine grease
and the steel dust and their smells
and the smell of the steel mill furnaces and of the exhaust of the
steel mill forklifts,
the sweetest moment
was always lifting that first can of beer
to my lips as I sat down in a chair at a window
in the sun and looked out
at the city of asphalt and stucco walls and knew
that all of that sweating
in all of that grease and oil and stink
had kept something alive inside of me,
something clean
and pure that burst out in smiles on my face and waited
to be put down
on the page,
something that would have been long dead
if I had ever taken that college degree job
in that immaculate white shirt.

A Little Bit of Heaven

Minimum wage
was an honor and I wore my badge of shabby
hole-ridden wearing-out T-shirt and jeans
with pride no one
made less money than I and I could sit
in a cheaply-furnished dive apartment among dying
alcoholics and old people
at a window drunk each Saturday night feeling
blessed and saintly like all of mankind
were my friend like
I could go anywhere and not owe one thing
to anyone like I was
free like I was in heaven
though I didn't have enough gas in my car to get me anywhere
but to and from work 5 days a week.
For one Saturday night
a week I could sit drunk at a window looking out
and feel
better about the money I made than I ever would
again.

No Choice

Standing on the wooden platform in front of my machine
I'd put my arms up between my machine and workbench,
one hand grabbing the top of my workbench backboard
and the other clutching onto the edge of the cold steel table
of my machine,
and I'd hang
with arms spread wide like Jesus on the cross
as my machine fed steel into a cutter
until
the Mexican at the Blanchard grinder in the corner
came over to ask me
if I was a religious man
and stare at me
until I let my arms fall and told him, 'No'
and I'd wait a while and then put my arms back
up as the pounding screaming teeth-jarring
noise and the shuddering concrete floor and the heat and stink
of the steel mill and the constant sadistic looks and laughs
and words
of the workers and the foreman and my
throbbing hangover pushed me
to climb a cross and be Jesus
rather than pick up a hammer or a wrench
and kill someone.

Coward

The men dying of industrial diseases the men
clench-fisted and hunched like boxers glaring
out at me from under their hard hat brims with nothing
but silent anger were better
the worn-out bodies and minds of those men
who had nothing
but to meet the steel mill clench-jawed
and wrestle it down and spit on it
each day were better,
hungover and staggering and trembling
and talking to themselves after 20 or 30 years
in the steel mill they were better
than me who had the words the talent the inspiration
to write about it
but was too terrified to do so –
what ferocious magnificent fearless masterpieces
could they have written
if they'd had the tools I had?

Strength

I wanted to be as strong inside
as our bodies
that lifted and tossed and turned the steel blocks
and hammered the $^{1}/_{4}$-ton steel shanks and standards
across mill tables and gripped wrenches to pull
nuts down tight enough atop clamps
to hold heat-treated tool steel as it was chewed and cut up
by cutters I wanted to be as strong inside as our bodies
that withstood
the pounding shock waves of steel screaming and concrete shuddering
and compressors and furnaces roaring I wanted
to reach inside myself and pull out
one scream
or passion
or tear of joy
that was as real and strong as that I wanted
to be a writer.

Kin

The foreigners
were the machinists I could talk to the Old World
Italians Venezuelans Chileans the ones
who could only half speak English they had
a humanness I could trust as they
wished me well as they put their arms around my shoulders
as they gave me their machinist secrets they had learned over
the years
and let me use their special hand-made tooling fixtures and cutters
joyfully
as if I was their son or brother there was a light
of warmth in their eyes as they watched
me learn watched me succeed at my machine as if
there was no greater treasure and I felt
closer to them and seemed to know them
so much better
than all of the American machinists
I worked with.

Life Raft

I hung on
to my machine after burning up a mattress after
exploding an oven full of gas in my face during
years of wanting to die and drunken
chain-smoking carelessness, I came
to the steel mill and hung on
to the handles of my machine to the table
of my machine
as the machine cut steel down
into dies,
I hung
onto that machine as my fellow workers' eyes stared
at my melted glasses and singed eyebrows or my blistered arm
and accused me like I was a criminal,
that machine
was the only thing that could somehow carry me
through somehow
preserve me until I found a reason to live and I hung on
to that machine
until my fingers ached.

Political Science

As I looked straight ahead
at the cutter chewing through steel clamped to my machine table
and tried to concentrate on my own thoughts I tried
to put up a wall of an invisible force field
between myself and Merlin at the next machine but
Merlin
just kept staring through that wall and coming over
to my machine day after day
to tell me more and more details about that annual horseshoe-
pitching get-together he'd gone to,
the one where they had a beer truck the one advertised on his
T-shirt
the one given by his neighbors who took down the wooden fence
between their backyards each year to have it
until
I finally realized that his desire to break down my wall
was just as strong and legitimate
as my desire to put it up.

It was the first time I'd really understood democracy.

A Lot in Common

The blacks
were the machinists I could talk to,
the blacks
with their crazy coats and hats and their knives
on their hips that they flashed
at supervisors,
their screaming and dancing at their machines,
their crap-shooting on workbenches,
their lunchbreak
conversations about toolbox guns and
parking lot broken windshields
fit right in
with my 25-year-old
ex-hippie ex-acidhead ex-English literature graduate student
turned machinist
panic as we all glanced about nervously
with our wild
bugged-out eyes at the lunch table and rapped
about stabbings and alcoholism and heart attacks
and horse races.

Old Souls

The blacks
smoking cigars in baseball stadium bleachers
and standing on warehouse loading docks at dawn
and driving forklifts
and cradling auto parts black with grease in their hands in garages
and pushing carts
weighted with hundred-pound loads of cans and bottles down alleys
full of ruts and potholes
and sitting in toolcribs behind five-inch-thick catalogues
of tools
are as old
as the chains
of centuries ago,
as old
as the first slave,
as the first blood under a whip and the first jerk
of a neck in a noose,
as the first man killed,
as the first man beaten by his brother,
as the first taking
of a man's dignity,
as the first foundation of the first
city,
as they look out at us with eyes full of something
as old as the first pain
flesh ever felt.

Termination

Feeling the vibrations coming out of the machines
with his palm flat against them,
and leaning his good ear
close to the green sides of the machines,
listening for the gears and shafts
turning in the guts of the machines,
listening for things only he
knew to listen for,
the foreman's whole body was aware
as the machines poured their decades of secrets
into his hand and ear
and he knew,
he knew what would happen to each of them,
whether there would be an accident
or whether it was all right.
His hands and jaw trembled slightly
from the 25 years
of the roars and shudders and chatterings
of steel mill drop hammers and presses and grinding wheels,
but he was still strong.

But the new hotshot manager and the machine operator
who wanted to be foreman
were into speed,
and the foreman took too long with his hand and ear
trying to keep machine cutters from blowing up in operators' faces,
so they rode him
until
each morning when he came to work and put his hard hat on
there seemed to be a heavier weight on his head,
pushing him into the concrete floor
of the steel mill,
driving his neck and his head
down into his shoulders
as if he were a shaft being driven down through concrete
by a jackhammer,
the trembling growing in his fingers
and jaws
until he had a stroke
that stopped the trembling and him
for good.

That manager and machine operator
really knew how to get the job done.

81

Unsightly

Shop floors
black with machine grease and pitted with potholes making forklifts
rock as they roll over them shop floors
with trails ground into them by the heels of machinists
operating the same machines for 20 years shop floors
making the toe
and knee and leg and hip bones
of workers ache with years and years on their concrete hardness shop
floors soaked with the blood of severed fingers and hands shop floors
where men have grown old
giving their best to make parts so buses
or wheelchairs could roll or planes fly or jackhammers pound shop floors
spat on and kicked and smashed with dropped loads
and gouged with crowbars
and covered with metal chips and stained with rust and oil shop floors
never shown in a company catalogue or photo shop floors
where we spend our lives.

Enterprise

The foreman's eyes letting a machinist know
that he will fire him whenever he feels like it all the workers
on the streets who cannot find work all
the cops ready to take them to County Jail all the machinists
racing to turn machine handles to turn out parts
faster than each other so they won't end up
out on the street all
the nightmares
and fear that never lets a man rest
or feel easy all
the stories of crazy bosses ruining lives all
the heart attacks
and fights
and murders and suicides
on machine shop floors all the lifeblood
making the engine that builds our world
race.

Broken

Laid off,
in a little trailer by a guard gate the machinists
are stripped
of tools out of their toolboxes
and photo ID badges
and company shirts,
stripped
of incomes,
stripped
of usefulness at 45 or 51 or 55
years old,
stripped
and sent out the gate like little boys,
little boys
with families
and mortgages
and lifetimes of pride
on the line
who must now beg
other companies for the right
to be adults.

Doing Time

Without jobs
their souls are strung up to hang
pointless and helpless as their bodies pace and stumble
and drive aimlessly around and their mouths
scream indignation and succor themselves
with bottles
of beer and booze without jobs they watch the shadows of palm
trees creep across the street and yards as they sit
in chairs they have fallen into with their heads hung down
day after day without jobs
they wrap their arms around themselves
and withdraw from everyone a thousand miles away
inside themselves to keep from going berserk
and attacking someone without jobs
all they can do is sit as if the whole world
around them was a jail cell they were waiting
to get out of.

Outside

After a year
unemployed the alley
begins to reach right up into your apartment and each
bang of beer and pop cans against the walls of garbage cans
by street people in the alley filling
shopping carts and bags for recycling center
dimes resounds
inside your apartment as you
can no longer ignore the street people as you walk the alley
and
can't help looking deeply into their eyes and realizing
that they're no different than you as
your bank account drops toward zero
and your apartment walls thin down to the thickness of paper
and the alley
seems to run right through your apartment as you begin to hate
the walls
and the gates and locks.

Community

The poor
sit on porches or on sofas placed out on
front lawns and talk
to each other and to people walking by on the sidewalk they stand around
for hours and hours in backyards and talk to each other they meet
in alleys where they talk
to each other or maybe give the poorer
of each other a quarter or 2 they cross streets wrapped in blankets
and homeless to greet each other the poor
gather in apartments or houses or garages to live
together and make cheap rents and have a roof
over their heads and they travel together
crammed into vans and big old cars with their arms and feet
sticking out of windows the poor
cannot afford to not talk to each other
to not know each other to not be human
to each other like
the rich can.

Intellectuals

The fingers
of jobless dying alcoholics
moving chess pieces on boards that are all they have
in single apartment rooms
or jails
or downtown chess clubs
or in parks these men
sitting Buddha-like crouched over the boards glad
for this gift from the gods this way
of passing time this way
of fingering and holding and moving
pieces of something meaningful
and beautiful and brilliant and maybe somehow cosmic
as the city
all around waits for them to die and gives them
nothing.

Now Is When Einstein Shatters the Universe with His Mind

Now
is when you must do whatever you must do now
is when Christ hangs on the cross now
is when anything might happen now
the ant
stops on the rock in the blazing mountain sun
and a monk
has no thoughts sitting on a bare floor
for half an hour now
we are alive now the breath moves in and out of our lungs and now
is when railroad tracks are laid across a continent now
a telescope revolves about the earth
and a machinist sets a dial on a machine to bore a perfect cavity
through the casing of a jackhammer now
is all the love that we will ever know
and every doomsday
and revolution
there will ever be and now
is when you will arrive for your 11:50 a.m. dental
appointment now
the phones are ringing
and the crows are cawing
and the chess player figures a way to move a pawn across the board
to take a queen
and the rain drips off the helmet of a soldier
who will tie Dostoyevsky to the firing squad stake
and the triangle
is thought of for the first time
and you put your foot down
on the sidewalk and get off
the bus now
is all
we have.

25 Vending Machine Candy Bars to Choose From

Why do we not live naked in caves in harmony with the universe
like all the other animals?
Is it to stand at a bank teller window at 9 am?
Is it to have walls between each other,
to drive to a factory 10,000 times in a life without really
knowing why,
to watch an apple fall
and think of gravity
or wind a watch on an airplane
or crush a man's hand
to gain a confession
or build the tallest monument on earth to yourself
or blow up a mountain
or fill a sea with filth
or strike terror into millions with a word,
why
are we the only animals on earth to put on clothes
and build sewer systems and think
of things to do?
Is it to count the days
and take photographs of each other
and try to beat each other to the ribbon in 100-yard dashes?
Is it to invent the can opener
or stand on a corner with your hand out hungry and have
thousands of cars pass you by?
Is it to hang like a fly in a spiderweb watching death creep
closer and closer in a retirement home?
Is it to pull the wings off a butterfly
or know how the valves in the heart work,
or is it to listen
to the ninth symphony of Beethoven
or stand before the Pietà of Michelangelo
or lie in the grass and read Walt Whitman,
trying to recapture a little bit of all
we have lost?

Bared Souls

These are real people as real
as the lines of years of worry and rage etched
into their faces as real
as a Marshall's eviction notice taped to a front door
or a pink termination slip
from a job that just paid someone enough to make the rent
each month as real
as the old chipped-paint hoods thrown open on
broken-down cars and
concrete corner curbs stood on all day with a piece of cardboard
begging for food as real
as sitting at a table staring out a window at the street
all day with no job and nothing
but a room and a 6-pack as real
as children screaming and running wild tearing up a house while welfare cutbacks
keep their mother buried under pillows in a bed afraid of everything
but darkness as real
as one man's fist suddenly cracking another man's cheek on a concrete
machine shop floor these people
do not have the luxury
of pretending.

Waste

All the bikers
who've cried like little babies in mental hospitals,
all the disowned children gone insane with loneliness
in apartments,
all the beautiful divorcees who've tried to kill themselves
because they felt so ugly inside all
the math geniuses with ravaged faces and no teeth
who've ridden rickety bicycles around slum blocks looking for dope
at 40,
all of the machinists gone slowly crazy
from the effects of Agent Orange,
all of the homeless women
who've shivered in alleys at 3 am,
all of the brilliant poets
who've died penniless beside emptied vodka bottles in their 30s,
all
once little kids
who jumped and shouted with joy.

It seems the earth should shudder
and scream out
because it must hold them all
in their graves.

When All the Electric Lightbulbs in the World Won't Help

The sun goes down
on men
with nowhere left to turn and women
with eyes black from the fists of their men the sun goes down
on children
with nothing for Christmas and the man
who is weeping in a corner because
he believes he is a failure the sun goes down
on the twisted aching backs
and hands of aging workers ready to fall asleep
an hour after making it home from the factory
and their cars
faded and dented and on their last legs
in the streets the sun goes down
as suicidal welfare mothers
hide their heads under pillows and homeless
men who used to own homes put their arms around themselves and shiver
against walls in alleys the sun goes down
on men with nothing but chess pieces
on chessboards in parks
and disowned 17-year-olds in strange cities thousands of miles
from home it does not pause
for one millionth of a second but goes down
on the man
spending seven days a week packing boxes on an assembly line who wanted
nothing but to be a painter and the bitter
drunken ex-minor-league baseball player who never made it
to the majors and all the women
staying out of the streets by hanging on
to men they don't love the sun goes down
like it did a billion years ago
as fading women switch on lights above mirrors and find
new lines in their faces and the muscles
of old boxers wither
and glaring billboard lights advertizing cigarettes and whiskey
come on all over the city and big
strong men finally realizing their women will never come back to them
drain bottles and break down
and cry the sun goes down
on 60-year-old men just fired with final paychecks in their hands
and no pensions and everywhere
people sit in dark rooms
without one dream left
to light their lives.

As Chairs Begin to Crack and Fall Apart Under Us

We sit waiting
for the Dodgers to win the pennant
and for brothers who have not called in years
to call
and for Christ to come back for
the oceans to die the bomb to drop we grip
the arms of old chairs bored watching TV show after TV show
all day waiting
to win the lottery waiting
for hangovers to go away for
broken toenails to grow back waiting
to be laid off
again we grip the arms of old chairs worn down by our hands and wait
for heart attacks and cancer and pay cuts
and plant closures
and for asshole relatives to call us again so we can scream at them we
wait to re-pot plants
and for the Queen Mary to blow her smokestack whistle at 10:00 a.m. and
for everything our 4th grade school teachers predicted about us
to come true for
a lover or a rock star or a politician to come into our lives
and save us as we grip the arms of old chairs
and watch boring TV shows
that are all we have.

The River

Blues music
is the rage
of every man fired for no good reason and the tears
of every woman beaten and every
baby born and every
man pushed toward nervous breakdown by a steel mill
roaring and shaking with noise and the rage of every man
talked to like a 5-year-old child by a boss blues music is
the car coming out of nowhere slamming
into your car and giving you paralysis
for life it is
ice cold rainwater pouring down on a homeless man in an alley
at 1 am and
the cries of pain of thousands of years
of slaves and
every hand unjustly manacled and the endless shuffling
of the homeless toward nothing as they circle blocks
for years blues music
is the hopeless silent cry of agony and rage
of anyone ever feeling that they could not make it through another day.

It is bigger than all of us and it will flow on
after we are dead and that
is its beauty.

Disowned

Just because the cold asphalt of an alley has been his bed
does not mean we will let him stand on our doorstep just because
he is forced to roam the streets all day as an animal
does not mean that
we must remember when he was not one just because
he must beg on streetcorners with no one in the world who cares about him
does not mean that
he can come to us for help just because
he has been stripped of dignity and privacy and hope
does not mean that we must
feel sorry for him just because
he has ccme back to us
doesn't mean that we have to see him or talk to him
or let him in just because
he was once a part of the family of man
does not mean he is
anymore.

As Our Money Runs Out

Laid off from our jobs we lie on beautiful white beaches in the sun
and pray
to be back in dark machine shops stinking of ground steel and
smoking oil,
laid off from our jobs we sit
under beautiful century-old trees in peaceful backyards praying
that we will once again stand
in front of nachines on filthy concrete floors
where no green thing will ever grow,
laid off from our jobs we lie
next to beautiful wives on beds where we could make love
for days
and pray
that we will soon be back in machine shops
where sweaty men in tank tops
slap and goose us with greasy fingers,
laid off from our jobs we sit
on surfboards under vast blue skies with nothing to do
but feel the ancient majesty of the sea
carry us on graceful ride after graceful ride
all day,
and pray
that we will soon be back
inside the windowless tin walls
of 30 x 50-foot machine shops
where merciless bosses have us by the balls as they pay us
peanuts.

Feasting

Interviewing,
the foreman
can really lean back in his leather swivel chair
with the supreme superiority and confidence of a man
holding all the cards and smile
down at us 100 or 200 machinists filing through his office
in this Los Angeles depression desperate
to be hired to fill his one open machinist position,
smile
down at us and feel how good the soft leather feels
against his back as we spill
our lives' qualifications across his desk and he picks them apart
and tells us how they don't quite fit
with all of the absolute and exact requirements he expects his
machinist to fill,
as he yawns and cleans his fingernails and narrows his eyes
like a cat zeroing in on the kill,
smiling
and waiting for that perfect applicant that will eventually appear
and be willing to work for less than he's worth.

I Know This Man

In the alley
I meet him:
a man who has had his humanity stripped from him
a man who has had his sanity stripped from him,
his wife
and his 42 years of dignity
stripped from him,
all the love and care of his mother and father
wasted,
all the child who was once 6 and had every present he could wish for
under the Christmas tree
gone
in him.
Invisible,
he lifts lids and picks through garbage,
keeps his eyes on the ground and scurries
along walls like an animal,
and all
the finest most brilliant arguments in the world
will never convince me that he deserves to be there,
for he is me
if I had not somehow stumbled across that job
it was the luckiest day of my life
to find.

As Executives in $1,000 Suits Get Bonuses

We work
decade after decade as our companies
lay off and hire and lay off and hire
and change philosophies and presidents and company logos and the colors
of our ID badges,
we grab
the same handles to the same machines making the same
parts
as our companies
merge
or move operations overseas
or eliminate departments by sending their work out
to vendors who pay their machinists
half as much,
we shrug
as the rumors fly about our shops
and our jobs and lives hang in the balance,
we plant our feet
firmly on concrete floors and hang onto those machine handles
and do our jobs,
sweating the same sweat
workers have always sweat
and aching to our bones
the way workers have always ached
and laying down our lives
the way workers have always laid them down,
the only things
that never change.

The World in Our Hands

We hold
in our hands for brief moments the train wheels
or aircraft wing actuators
or bulldozer teeth
we have cut out of metal,
as we lift the sharp shine of their precisely cut
edges dripping with cutting oil
off of our machine tables.
Before they are painted
and stamped with company names and sold
in a marketplace that keeps some men
in luxury cars and suits and others
living in sidewalk houses of cardboard,
for the briefest of moments we hold
these keys to the engine that drives the world
in our hands,
wishing
that somehow
we could make the world
as pure and beautiful and right as these raw parts feel
in our hands
before we give them up
and stack them in the steel bins of the companies.

Premature

Recalled
to Goodstone Aircraft Company I eagerly enter building 100
to report to PARKING CONTROL where
I expect to receive a parking sticker for my car,
giving
the lady behind the desk my employee no. 824921
and waiting as she scans her computer screen.
She frowns
and shakes her head at her failure to find me on her screen
and wheels away from her screen in her swivel chair and tells me to come
back Monday, saying, 'You don't exist yet!'

It appears that while I was away
Goodstone's powers
have grown even more God-like.

Adjusting

We machinists
spend 15 minutes wandering around in and out of building 89 because
we were told the wrong room to go to for our hearing protection class.
When we finally are directed to the right room we find
there is another class in it and so
must wander around for 20 minutes more until
we finally go into the room to sit down where
we wait 15 more minutes
for the instructor who is late.
But,
having been just recently recalled to Goodstone Aircraft Company
after a year or 2 laid off and unemployed and unable to find decent work
in the depressed economy we machinists
don't say any of the disgruntled or snide words
we would have said before being laid off.
Instead, we think about the $20 an hour we are making
and settle back in the plush chairs and listen
to each other's old inane boring remarks and old-as-the-dust-in-the-hills
jokes
and stare at the walls and twiddle our thumbs
with big smiles and chuckles and laughs of delight.

We're going to learn to love Goodstone Aircraft Company
yet.

Control Control

If you are not coming to work you must call
Absence Control,
if you are bringing any kind of guest through the gates into the plant
you must first consult
Security Control,
if you need a new ID badge you must go to
Badge Control,
if you need a parking sticker you must go to
Parking Control,
when you receive a new job it is off a rack stocked
by Production Control and when you are done machining the job
it must be inspected at
Quality Control.

At Goodstone Aircraft Company control
is out of control.

Icons

Dick the machinist
who was 18 in 1957 wears his hair
perfectly combed in a sculpted pompadour
with that perfect curl hanging down in front
of his forehead and Mears the machinist
who was 18 in 1968 wears his sideburns
down to his jowls and a huge
handlebar moustache while Ron
who was 18
in 1977 has a wild heavy metal growth of permed hair
shooting out in all directions and hanging down to his waist.
Each of these machinists
it seems will immortalize down to his death
the era of his prime,
while biker machinists
of all ages and all eras back to WW2
strut about still 18 in those timeless black leather jackets
and 2-foot-long mountain man beards.

101

Good Workmanship

I called the supervisor
over to my workbench to tell him
with head hung down that I had scrapped out
2 aluminum parts and so now
there were 6 bad aluminum parts out of a total of 13
aluminum parts on the manufacturing order,
wincing inside
as I expected rage and distress
and reprimand.

But the supervisor
just smiled a very weird kind of smile and told me
to quickly
take all those parts down to the saw and cut them up
into little pieces and bury them in different corners
of the 4 different bins
full of odd pieces and chunks of aluminum,
while he had the manufacturing order
downgraded to just 7 parts.

Now I could understand
our department's phenomenally low scrap rate
a little better.

Above Us

The supervisor
is good at lifting his nose into the air and yelling,
'MIIISTER Voss, MIIISTER Jackson, MIIISTER Miller...'
at whichever of us machinists he is mad at, pointing
his finger ominously toward the door in the tin wall
and shouting, 'OutSIIIDE!!'
indicating
that we must go outside to be reprimanded.
He is good
at keeping the expensive dress suit he wears around
the machine shop immaculate and giving us sinister
scowling dirty looks whenever we seem to be beginning
to think that he likes us
and he is good at making us keep the rubber mat carpet
leading out of his office clean
of every last speck of metal chips.

He would have no trouble at all
wearing a crown.

Cutting Away the Fat

Over in building 70
are the Z-330 Transport Plane tooling fixtures
with beams 30 feet high, fixtures
the size of basketball courts in which sit sections
of Z-330 fuselages being riveted and wired, fixtures
that rest on computerized platforms at dozens
of points, computerized platforms
that can be moved and tilted on 5 axes to adjust the Z-330
fuselages in a myriad
of positions computer calculated
and as hair-trigger fine-tuned and complex
as advanced calculus,
while all around these fixtures
work the assemblers riveting and wiring,
assemblers whose ranks keep getting thinner and thinner
as they are laid off
so that Goodstone Aircraft Company
can compete in today's economic landscape
of stripped-down-to-the-bone
leanness.

Not Impressed

The veterans
at their old manual machines surrounded
by all of the new computer-controlled machines
furiously crank handles lifting and lowering the beds of
their machines and furiously crank handles moving
their machine tables in and out and back and forth.
They furiously and agilely
crank their machines' universal heads into angles on 2 axes
to put cutters on compound angles for extra-complex
cuts and sweat
and smile happily.
Lifting their index fingers in the air
they look contemptuously over at the computer machine
operators and nod
signifying
the single act
of pushing the 'Cycle Start' button
which the computer machine operators are required
to perform in order for their computer machines to
automatically produce
aircraft parts.

Politics

Harry
is willing to work through breaks and lunch
doing whatever obnoxious impossibly difficult unreasonably
urgent job the supervisor wants him to do
if it will make the supervisor look good.
The other machinists
always proudly
take their legal union-negotiated breaks and lunches
and refuse to do unreasonable jobs just because the
supervisor tries to shove them down their throats.
They end up
working their butts off as the supervisor relentlessly
hovers about them and turns the feed and speed controls
on their machines up and relentlessly harasses them
about leaving their work area.
Harry, on the other hand,
spends 95% of his time kicked back
in a leather swivel chair in front of his machine
daydreaming
or walking
around the shop bugging other machinists
or reading the newspaper
in a bathroom stall.

At Goodstone Aircraft Company,
being naive
just doesn't pay.

Ticker Tape Parade

He came back in
one day through the narrow door cut out in the tin wall
of the steel mill to say hello
to all of us machinists, making the rounds
to shake all of the hands with a big smile when we all knew
that he had brown lung from
sucking in all that steel dust while operating
that grinding machine over in the corner for 25 years
without a respirator, he strutted
and beamed and grinned to be back
for 10 minutes in the shop he had retired from
a year ago,
dying and proud to be
in the place he had given his life for as we stared
at him wishing we could think of him as a hero
rather than a victim.

Mental Patient

The supervisor hovers about,
periodically shaking Rick
and screaming 'Earth to Rick! Earth to Rick!'
into his ear.
Rick moves and laughs and flexes his fingers
and follows the path of his machine's cut
for a minute or two,
until he stops halfway through a swivel
in his leather chair
and his eyes are suddenly glazed again
and he has gone back
to that place no one else knows anything about,
as he sits transfixed and a million miles away,
his machine turning automatically
through a 40- or 50- or 60-minute cut,
the supervisor hovering and shaking him and screaming,
glad to take care of someone
with such an exceptional talent
for never getting bored,
no matter how monotonous and mindless
a job gets.

Lingo

After years and years in machine shops,
machinists begin to talk less and less.
Instead, they begin to
tap their rubber or lead or ball-peen hammers
against their machines,
learning how to play their machines like steel drums.
They walk around with big sheets of sheet metal,
bending and buckling them
until they whirr and hum
like weird high-tech
guitar solos.
They line up cutter holders of varying diameters
and play them like organ pipes
by sticking the tips of their airguns into them
and blasting air through them,
or they blast air against the insides of their closed
fists and create kazoo-like sounds
by rubbing and opening and closing their fingers
and thumbs –

until occasionally, when they are really inspired,
they break out in vocals
to lead their own one-man bands –
the Italians singing opera,
the Mexicans mariachi,
and the bikers
heavy metal.

Fringe Benefit

The janitor towed lines of dumpsters
up and down the machine shop aisles,
across the loose steel plates
that covered the scrap-metal conveyor belts
under the aisles.

The janitor nodded with booze as he drove,
tipping forward and sideways
in the towmotor seat,
leaning like he was about to fall out,
his eyes red and barely open.

But he made the machine shop explode
with the pops and bangs and cracks
of the steel dumpsters jarring and bouncing
across the steel plates
as he drove the towmotor FAST
down the aisles.

Not only did this keep him awake,
it helped ruin the already raw nerves
of the machine shop supervisors.

Every job has its rewards.

Uptight

Bob tightens the nuts
down onto the clamps.
He is grunting and grimacing,
his biceps straining
and his back nearly wrenching out
as he turns red and tugs on a 2-foot-long crescent wrench,
digging his boot heels into the concrete floor.
He gets out a 4-foot-long section of steel pipe
and slips it over the crescent wrench,
grabbing the pipe as if it were an oar,
leaning back,
giving 4 final tugs
that make the nuts and bolts creak
as if they are about to snap.

The slab of aluminum he must cut is now anchored
to the machine table with more than twice the torque
required to keep extremely hard heat-treated
tool steel
from moving under the force of cutting.

Bob doesn't want that son-of-a-bitch
on night shift
to think that he can tighten nuts
tighter than Bob can.

Our Leader

Insubordination
is the supervisor's favorite word his eyes flare
as he fires it out of his mouth
at us machinists whenever he can.
Not writing down our names on the roll-call sheet
during one of his shop talks
is insubordination,
not going outside to get our ass chewed out
for laughing at him
is insubordination and not following
any of his insane, incompetent, self-defeating and insulting
orders to the exact letter
is insubordination.

How else can he gain our respect?

The Perfect Woman

Machinists
strut about their machines as if those machines were their
women they stick their chests out
and light big cigars and boom out brags
in loud boisterous voices
in front of them as if
those machines had given them the best fuck
or blowjob of their life a fuck or blowjob
that no woman could ever equal as they
strut about the machines stroking and polishing and oiling
them, knowing
that those machines are better than any woman because they
will never talk back to them.

Mingling with the Little People

Seeing the company president
not only coming out of the office building to actually
walk around the machine shop
and look at us work,
but SMILING
from ear to ear in his 3-piece-suit
as he did it,
had me puzzled until
3 days later the entire nightshift
and much of the dayshift
machinists were eliminated in a massive layoff.

He'd been calculating.

Evil

There was one thing
we machinists feared from supervisor Keal
more than Keal's
screaming fits of rage more than his
suspicious spying or his demeaning
cruel insults or his nerve-racking derogatory lectures against the fence
outside the machine shop wall or his threats
to reprimand or write up or suspend or fire or jail
us machinists,
and that was
his smile,
his special friendly and heartwarming
smile with maybe a squeeze on the arm
or a hug around the shoulder:

it meant
that he had truly marked you
for destruction.

A Lesson I'll Never Forget

The job
came in one of those green folders which meant
it had been run before as a 'PFP' or 'Proven For Production' job and thus was
100% guaranteed proven
to work smoothly and perfectly and I
loaded the 'proven for production' program into my machine's computer memory
and loaded a 12 x 7-inch slab of aluminum
into the vise and turned up the feed dial to 100% just like
the 'proven for production' job instruction sheet said to do
and punched the Cycle Start button
on the Computer Controls box and watched
the cutter rip into the slab of aluminum which hung
in the air between the vise jaws and began
to tremble as the cutter began
to scream and I watched
full of 'proven for production' confidence until
the slab shook and popped loose
from the vise jaws and was grabbed and spun
by the cutter faster and faster until it approached
1000 rpm until
I finally staggered to the control box to slam the edge of my fist
into that huge red 'EMERGENCY STOP' button
just in time
to keep the cutter from hurling the aluminum slab like a razor-sharp discus
at 100 mph
and maybe cutting me in half.

At Goodstone Aircraft Company
naivete
can be deadly.

In Top Shape

As part of its stripping down to a 'lean and mean'
status
Goodstone Aircraft Company has closed
2 of its plants and moved all of the tools and instruments
and cutters from its tool cribs in those plants
over to the tool crib in our plant where
the tools and instruments and cutters
sit stacked in chaotic piles and thrown together haphazardly
in unmarked boxes and stuffed
randomly into upstairs drawers and cabinets
where they can never be found for us machinists
by the one lone tool crib attendant who is left
after Goodstone laid off the rest of them
in yet another step in its relentless march
toward supreme stripped down
competitive efficiency.

Out of Touch

The machinists
who always had those nice
benevolent everything-couldn't-be-peachier
smiles
on their faces as they ran their machines and walked around the
building all day with peaceful twinkling eyes no matter how
obnoxious or insane things got at Goodstone Aircraft Company,
were the ones you had to watch the ones
who were liable
to suddenly break someone's cheek with a coldcock punch
or pull out a gun
or go insane in a bathroom stall.

It just isn't healthy
to be that far removed from reality.

Power Failure

Every so often
a Computer Numerically Controlled milling machine
that has operated perfertly smoothly for months and months,
allowing its operators
loading time-tested programs into it
to lean back in leather swivel chairs half-asleep
reading or daydreaming for 8 hour shifts,
will suddenly
and without one iota of warning
blow a power unit in its main panel causing
the machine to go into a 3-axis
rapid-travel
dive of the head and its spinning razor-sharp cutter down
toward the table,
as the apoplectic
adrenalin-crazed near-heart-attack
machinist
finally manages to whip the Feed Control knob down to zero
which does no good
and then
slams the side of his fist into the big red Emergency Stop button
which does no good
as the cutter and machine head inexorably dive downward
and crash and twist and explode into vise
and part and angle plate and machine table.

The gods still have ways of punishing men
who think they've got it made.

Phobia

Supervisors
have many ways of letting a machinist know
that they are displeased they
twitch and jerk their shoulders about inside their coats
and rattle their keys angrily in their pants pockets
and pace back and forth red-faced
with lowered brows or huffing and puffing cheeks
or ball their fists up in their pants pockets
and pump themselves up and down on the balls of their feet
like they want to hit a machinist they
glare and frown and jab their fingers in the air
frantically to make sure
that the thing they fear the most in all the world
does not happen:
a machinist feeling that he is doing a good job.

Never Say Die

There is always one
in every machine shop one
machinist who rips a dustpan off the wall
like he was a soldier in battle ripping his sword
out of its scabbard who
makes musical instruments out of parts or holders
by holding them to his mouth and dancing around blowing through
them like a jazz improvisor who
plays his machine like a steel drum circling it
with a big rubber hammer pounding out melodies
by knowing exactly which points and thicknesses of steel
to hit on the machine who rides the handcarts
around and around the workbenches and machines
laughing and giggling like a little kid
on his first scooter.

There is always one machinist who just refuses to believe
that he's at work.

The Vice-President Gives His Monthly Shop Talk

The vice-president smiles
and wants the machinists to smile,
as he holds the company jackhammers
up into the air,
but the machinists are not paid to smile.
They do not give a fuck about the company
jackhammers
and he knows it.
He knows it
and they know that he knows it
and he knows that they know that he knows it.
He holds the company jackhammers
up into the air
and talks
as if he were really excited and delighted
about the way the company jackhammers break up concrete.

And he knows that the machinists know
that this is the one time each month
when their jobs look a lot better than his.

Corrective Action

We machinists
complain that the reason
we have to hoard cutters
in the drawers of the cabinets by our machines
is because we can so seldom count
on getting them from the tool crib.

But the tool crib tells us
that the reason we can so seldom get them from the tool crib
is because we hoard them.

So,
the tool crib sends a man around with a cart
to collect every last cutter out of every one of our cabinet
drawers
and put them into big plastic trays
so that Goodstone Aircraft Company can sell them for next to nothing
at auction.

I guess that will teach us to complain.

Realist

Mick
on the machine next to mine gets offended
if I don't look at him or talk back to him
as he shouts his life story over at me for the third time.
'IGNORING me, huh?!' he'll shout
over at me indignantly
with his hands on his hips as his cutter plows through steel,
but if
I listen intently to everything he says
as I try to run my machine
and nod my head and say 'Yeah' a lot in sympathy and agreement
with his opinions and feelings
he'll stop and jab his finger in the air toward me
and shout indignantly, 'HUMORING me, eh?!'
Then,
if I start to disagree with or question his remarks or come back
with barbed contradictory views of my own he'll
stomp around on the platform in front of his machine swinging his fists
and shout, 'Getting SURLY with me, huh?!!'

No one is going to try to pull the wool over Mick's eyes
by pretending they can get along with him.

Reborn

Carl
worked one of the 2-ton drop hammers he placed
forgings under the hammer and then flipped them over
with 2-foot-long steel tongs
as the hammer came smashing down from 20 feet above
twice in rapid succession making
the concrete floor shudder under Carl's steel-toed boots
with each deafening pound,
Carl's arms and hands
trembling but Carl smiling,
making his money in front of that hammer
and flipping through all of his pussy magazines
during breaks as he
showed everyone those big worm-like scars across his
wrist,
he'd almost killed himself and now
he was back and giving thumbs-up signs and
smiling big smiles all the time he had
a 2-ton drop hammer and pussy magazines and life
just didn't get much better.

T.G.I.F.

After work each Friday
the workers celebrate the end of the work week
by rushing to their cars
and throwing open the doors,
denting the doors of the cars next to them,
the drivers of the dented cars
climbing out
and kicking dents into the offenders' doors.
The workers who make it out of the parking lot right away
rear-end
and sideswipe each other in the street,
and keep on going,
cursing and shaking fists and revving their engines
and jockeying for position
to get to the boulevard –
terrorizing and periodically running over
any workers foolish enough to forego cars
and attempt to cross the street on foot
to get to the buses.

Nights

Night shift
attracts the old men machinists with dead wives
the lonely divorced
machinists the dreamy
withdrawn misfit and alcoholic and druggie machinists
who
want to escape
the day shift with its machinists all full of piss and vinegar racing
and competing with each other night shift
is beautiful
with its machinists who only want to hide and be left alone
with their machines who only want
to survive
and drive home through dark deserted
ambitionless streets.

Wallflowers

There are some machinists
who never seem to want to take their eyes off their machines,
who hover
around their machines at all times hiding behind them
and hugging
close to them in their leather chairs staring
at cutters making thousands of identical turns slicing back and
forth through blocks of steel
like it was the most fascinating thing they had ever seen,
who when
they happen to look out across the machine shop at other machinists
drop their mouths open
like they were from another planet and had never seen a human
being before, then jerk
their eyes quickly and desperately back toward their machines
that they know
they can trust.

Lucky

We had it as good as we could get it
working in that steel mill,
as good a job
as we could find as we shuffled
in our steel-toed boots and hard hats and charcoal-tinted face
shields and leather gloves all night
shoving 20-foot bars of steel across roller stands in and out
of the mouths
of blast furnaces
and cutting shanks out of the bars' glowing orange tips
as we sucked the air
hot like a branding iron and stinking of steel dust
ground by a hundred hand grinder operators all around us
up our nostrils and down into our lungs
and watched the veteran steelworkers trembling with DTs
and decades of the pounding of drop hammers and the screaming
of automatic drill presses
stare at us 20-something-year-olds
like we were new meat
in jail,
we tried to feel happy that we had found as good a job as we
could find but really
when we thought about it very much
it made us want to cry.

Feelers

We machinists all
watched our fingers that were the tools of our trade that
held micrometers across machined parts and lightly turned
micrometer rods down to snug thousandth-of-an-inch measurements
that gingerly
adjusted parts in fixtures to tighten them down
indicated to absolute parallelism or perpendicularity that
wielded 50-pound lead hammers and 3-foot-long
steel socket wrenches hammering
$1/2$-ton parts into position and clamping them down,
we'd all
heard the stories about the fingers thrown 30 feet
through the air by cutters fingers
sliced off and still wiggling on machine tables and we all
saw the photos of hands with missing fingers
tacked to the 'Safety' section of the bulletin boards
and had gotten tools
from Lefty the tool crib man who had been a machinist
and whose right hand was missing 2 fingers,
and at the end of the day having cut off no fingers
we washed and dried those fingers
and wiggled them in the air and smiled thinking
about the schooners of beer and the breasts
they could all still fondle.

Carnegie Hall with Tin Walls

Using 10-ton cranes
to lower $1/4$-ton or $1/2$-ton parts
down onto milling machine tables the greatest machinists
use 30-pound lead hammers like baseball bats
to hammer steel parts
into position
with all the strength in their muscular backs and legs,
then clamp
them down with 3-foot-long socket wrenches
using every muscle in their hands
and forearms and chests as they tighten
steel hex-nuts down around bolts until
they squeal,
turning
machine dials to thousandth-of-an-inch calibration marks,
then crouching
over parts like surgeons
with outside micrometers and depth micrometers
and inside micrometers
after each thin-as-cellophane
machine cut
to with the lightest of touches in the very tips
of their fingers measure
with thousandth-of-an-inch to 10-thousandths-of-an-inch
accuracy
bored-out cavities or shaved surfaces,
until
from brute force
to the most delicate touch on earth,
they have played their bodies
like virtuosos
play pianos.

Select Company

My having hidden for 4 years inside my apartment
gave me
the prestigious air of the desperado as I worked in the steel
mill and the Mexican
came by my machine to stand beside me
and furtively slip the 2 bullets
he kept in his pants pocket out and show them to me like
I would understand and the 23-year-old machinist
who had been dropping acid since he was 11
came by to tell me that God was alive in the steel mill
and Mick the newlywed
trembling and walking in crazy jerks because of nerves
stepped near my ear and told me in low tones
how worried and pissed off he was that his wife
just lay there when he fucked her
and wouldn't give him a blowjob.

You just naturally hear from the cream of the crop
when you're as well thought of
as I was.

Brotherhood

To work
with men who had dropped out of high school who
couldn't read or write who
thought grabbing and goosing each other was the height of humor who
could stare at a wall or a piece of steel
for an hour and not get bored who
knew only
to feed their stomachs and their lust and thirst who
never ceased laughing and grinning with the joy of having a 10
or 30-minute workbreak who
were proud to lift and shove and roll and heat and cut
steel,
after I had dropped out of the U.C.L.A. Ph.D. program in
English literature,
seemed
the most beautiful privilege imaginable as
I found being human
more than enough
to have in common.

The Secret

I like the idea of men
who could have been math geniuses operating
drill presses in the corners of machine shops for 20 years because
they want nothing more
than women's bodies and creamy beer men
with the hearts of great poets who sit in steel cages
operating huge stinky spar mills because
it is enough for them to lie on a beach and stare up at a sky men
who might have been Beethoven
sitting at grinding wheels all their lives because
the sun striking the wooden bar they sit at every late afternoon
is enough for them men
who could have ruled the world with their cleverness
sitting with smiles and twinkly eyes
at milling machines because
they need nothing but weekends sitting on boards
like Buddhas
waiting for waves all day I like
to think of them laughing with their dirty hands and meager wages
like kings.

Creators

I wanted to be
with the steelworkers with the 40-year veteran trembling
in his hands and jaw from the noise and heat with
the bloodshot crazed eye of the alcoholic steelworker hungover
to make it another day with
the wild eye of the veteran of a thousand acid trips
or the ex-con
or mental patient who had to work in the steel mill
to survive I wanted to be
with the lungs sucking in steel dust with
the nerves breaking down and hearts failing
from the decades of pounding and slamming and shaking
and screaming and shattering of steel I wanted
to be with the man senselessly shouting out obscenities to make it
through another day with
the man covered with the black filth of the skin
of steel bars with the black sheep
thousands of miles from home who knew no one
and never spoke I wanted to be
with those sweating insomniacal ready-to-snap
always-at-the-end-of-their-rope
hanging-by-a-thread
minimum wage outcasts who still somehow managed to carry the world
on their shoulders.

Upside Down

In one wild
obscenity screamed at a 60-foot-high steel mill tin wall in one
stinking drop of sweat rolling down the ribs
of a pipe bending machine operator in one
jaw trembling with 30 years of the shock waves of torn and pounded steel
screaming and jarring into it like a jackhammer in one
eye crazed with 30 years of working the same machine throwing
the same switch turning the same wheel in one
Mexican who cannot speak one word of English staring at his
work with head bowed for 8 hours as if he were praying in one
finger
severed at the knuckle by a slamming punch press blade in one
tear
of rage burning in the eye of the machine operator forcing his mouth shut
as the foreman once again screams threats of firing at him
there is more
human dignity
than in the cleanest shiniest executive office floor
or the most polished executive desk
or smile
or handshake.

Living Bible

Crucifixes
around the necks of Mexican machine operators barely making enough
money
to live crowded together in apartments crucifixes
around the necks of machine shop floor sweepers
just up from skid row just up
from near-death drinking binges who sweep
oily burned stinking steel chips
across blackened concrete floors toward sawed-in-half-oil-drum
chip bins like it was the most sacred thing in the world crucifixes
around the necks of friendless familyless machine operators
who never speak to anyone who look up out of tortured lost eyes
like a crucifix
and a machine shop is all they have crucifixes
around the necks of Vietnam veterans
who sit in their chairs at their machines
twisted and pulled inward with arms thrown around themselves like
only a crucifix can keep them from killing themselves
and everyone around them these
are crucifixes that really
mean something.

Gypped

These aging
machinists putting in their last years
within walls they have worked within
for 30 or 40 years around machines
they have operated for 30 or 40 years as the flesh
droops more and more on their bones and their smiles and frowns
etch lines deeper and deeper into their faces and their moves
grow smoother and smoother in perfect artful repetitions
of what they have done for 30 or 40 years until
they seem to be dancing
with their machines with the controls and handles
and vises and cranes which are
lifetime partners,
dancing
to some priceless music inside themselves that has never been recognized
or rewarded
by the company and never will be
as they head
for that last paycheck and that cake and coffee party to walk out the gate
and disappear.

With Cutting Oil All Over His Hands

He works
way down the aisle 200 feet
from the rest of us machinists
on an antique drill press
surrounded by unused rusting manual machines,
68 years old
and hardly able to walk,
his chest crisscrossed
by all those open-heart surgery scars and his wife
just six months dead,
chain-smoking non-filter Camels,
and we wonder
when it will be that one of us
walking to the scrap bin or the saw in the back of the building one night
on the concrete floor blackened with decades of grimy heels
will find him
among his piles of spiralled steel drilling chips
two or three hours dead,
a man who had his toolbox and his steel-toed shoes
and his machine
and nothing else,
a man
who could some day
be any one of us.

Round 15

The aging
black machinist shuffles
around the machine shop,
his old
eyes buried in folds of wrinkled flesh sad
as his head hangs down and his legs
move
in stiff halting jerks like they have been beaten
and broken all over with a baseball bat as
he says nothing and stares at his feet,
though
sometimes he puts on
that Malcolm X T-shirt with that big photo of Malcolm X
and that big X on it,
and walks about the shop with his head up
as if to dare anyone to say anything about his wearing
that shirt,
as his eyes come alive just enough to let us know
that there is something inside him
that is not dead
yet.

Battlefield

Vietnam vets
who sit at their machines for weeks without saying one word
to another machinist who
stare at tin walls with arms thrown around themselves
for hours or pace
in front of their machines with sweaty furrowed brows
or pick up 100-pound vises and throw them around
or bury knives to the hilt throwing them into floorboards under their
feet like
they are not in the machine shop at all but
somewhere where the killing of human beings comes
very cheap Vietnam vets
at machines next to us who
stare at us like they don't know us like
they've never seen us before as they sweat and strain on the edge of
rampages
until we
who never had to go to that war feel
that we are finally
there.

A Long Road

The black
drill press machinist picked up the flyer
announcing the new Martin Luther King company holiday
off the bench in the machine shop and nodded
and touched it with his fingers
as his face registered how deeply he was moved and he said, 'That's
the man who made us free.'

And the white mill machine machinist
laughed
in disgust as soon as the black drill press operator turned his back,
and said, 'No. That's the guy that couldn't keep his mouth shut and so
they had to shoot him!'

Not quite free
yet.

Their Dream

Vietnamese
machinists hold their heads up extra high
as they strut
around the machine shop beaming with smiles
and giving thumbs up signs to the American machinists.
Until they try to talk.
Then
they snap their fingers and shake their fists angrily
as they stammer out the broken English words
that the American machinists rarely understand,
hanging their heads briefly
with doubt.
Until they raise them again
higher than the Americans have ever raised their heads,
breathing in the American air
of the machine shop as if it tastes good as they break out in those
beaming smiles again and shine them
on the Americans giving thumbs up signs
again high
with the hope that here in America
just being a human being
who can beam with smiles
is enough.

Making Up for It

Big men
with muscles and tattoos
operating 2-ton drop hammers
or 10-ton cranes who have
been unable to go on another day who have tried
to kill themselves and broken and cracked
in mental hospitals big men
swaggering and strutting up and down steel mill aisles with chests
puffed out
and $100 bills in their wallets who
love to grab
the ends of 20-foot bars of steel swinging above their heads
or stick
their face toward the smashing down of the 2-ton drop hammer making
the concrete floor under their feet quake
because
somewhere inside they are trembling
like little kids
afraid of the dark.

Providing a Service

We should have been grateful
to work in that gasket factory and feed fiberglass and asbestos
through presses that pounded down onto the cutting edges
of steel-rule dies we should have been grateful
for the tiny tin-walled bullding like an oven
with that diagram
on the wall of worker names in a pyramid leading toward the biker president
on top and the minimum wages
and working
on the 4th of July as the vice president threw cherry bombs
out of his door down the aisle between our presses we should have been grateful
for the floor-quaking pounding and the itch on our hands and arms and
all the fibers going up our noses and down into our lungs
and the way we sweat to make our quota of gaskets
and the boxing matches with the foreman
out in the parking lot during lunch we should have been grateful
we had jobs
and weren't in jail.

137

Tenderized

All of that muscle
in the hands of the steel mill veterans,
all of that muscle
in ribbons up and down their forearms and like steel cord
in their biceps and chests and backs and legs from
sticking poles down through holes in flats piled with steel and grabbing
the poles and hauling the flats
with one hand all those muscles
from wrestling 20-foot bars of steel hanging by cranes down
onto roller bars and
tossing
50-pound steel shanks into bins and wielding
50-pound lead hammers to smash steel slabs down
tight in vises now
strange
on these men nearing 50 or 60 who now
constantly tremble like weak kittens
in their jaws and fingertips
from too many decades of the roaring noise
and the pounding shock waves and
the million explosions of drill bits
and drop hammers and punch presses
against steel.

Food Chain

We machinists keep
our xerox copies of the seniority list under
the clear plastic sheets covering our workbenches
as the layoff rumors
circulate more and more around the shop,
hiding
behind our toolboxes atop the shelves above our workbenches
and running our fingers
again and again down the list of 40 or so names
to our own
and trying to tell ourselves that we will escape the axe,
that only
the men with less seniority under us on that list will get the axe
as we
furtively cast glances around our toolboxes at those we believe
will be gone,
not wanting them to see
how eagerly we calculate and cross out their names in our minds in order
to assure our own survival,
not wanting to have to face
ourselves
and what the company has made us become.

Ethical Giants

We machinists gather in the conference room
and view the Goodstone Aircraft Company interactive video
about ethics.
The video presents to us and asks us to discuss
the reasons why informing on our fellow employees
is the ethical thing to do,
why
our qualms about informing are not ethical,
giving us
many phone numbers to various managers and offices and ombudsmen
so that we may inform personally or anonymously
on behavior inconsistant with company rules
and thus maintain
the company's and our
ethical integrity.

Apparently Goodstone Aircraft Company
considers its filling up the office buildings with hundreds of air
conditioners
while the machine shop has none
and its consistent lying to us about our hard work preserving our jobs
and its filling of our building with toxic fumes
and its laying off of 50-year-old men
with families and mortgages
to the streets where there are no jobs
so that rich upper managers can get bonuses
highly ethical.

Don't Expect Any Apoligies

Machinists who are short
hold their heads up and scowl and strut about
throwing steel clamps and blocks around like they are 6-foot-5-inches-tall.
Machinists who limp
with clubfoots are always dragging them racing out the door at the end
of the shift cutting in front of people to get to their cars in the
parking lot before anyone else.
Vietnamese machinists
wear huge confident smiles
as they talk to the American machinists
in broken barely intelligible English
as if the American machinists were hanging on their every word.
Legally insane
machinists proudly boast of all the UFOs they have seen
and how the FBI is tapping their phone
and a nudist camp witch
putting spells on them,
while ex-cons
proudly boast that they have been in every jail in Southern California
as they regularly throw stools over the tops of machines
and explode in rages
like they might kill someone.

What might keep other people down
only gives a machinist the chance
to show how much balls he has.

Airborne

Goodstone Aircraft Company machinists
can't help walking around the shop occasionally
holding their arms out like airplane wings and making
big sweeping turns as they
glide down to land in the seats
of their leather chairs.
They can't resist taking those 2-foot-long thin steel flexible rulers
and holding them in the center with thumb and forefinger
and raising them above their heads and jiggling them
violently until their ends are flapping up and down
like beating wings as they move them up and down the aisle
like bats,
and when
some machinist has his 40th birthday one of the machinists may
come up to him with his arms out like
he is flying and then
drop one of his arms and go into a spinning dive
like an airplane crashing
just to show the turned-40 machinist what he has in store for him.

People who build airplanes all their lives
start to feel like them.

Another Slap in the Face

We department 517 machinists
are directed to a newly inaugurated awards program meeting by the manager
in building 41.
We assemble before a bulletin board on a chain-link fence in the main
aisle and shift our stances
and pick at our fingernails until one by one
each of us notices the big picture of Curly
with his goofy mop of permed hair
grinning at us from the center of the bulletin board
under a sign in big letters reading 'EMPLOYEE OF THE MONTH',
and one by one we
lower our heads and slap them with our hands and shake our heads
back and forth moaning and saying, 'It can't be true!' or
'I'm going to be sick!' as we jerk in mock wretching motions,
each of us remembering how Curly has for years kissed the ass of supervisors
by doing their pet jobs and then goofed off driving us crazy pestering
and teasing and tormenting us at our machines all day
while we tried to work,
each of us
turning toward the other to say things like, 'I wonder how much he paid
for it!' and, 'I wonder how many pairs of knee pads he had to wear out
to get it?'

Goodstone Aircraft Company
has found their perfect employee of the month.

One-Way Street

Sitting in the conference room
around the big table we machinists have listened
to the manager telling us for 20 minutes
that Goodstone Aircraft Company wants us machinists and Goodstone
to be a team,
that we must give all our skills and abilities
and energy and ideas
to running the machine shop better and faster
so that Goodstone can thrive,
when John raises his hand and says, 'What's with all this TEAM bullshit
when we never get NUTHIN' we request from Goodstone – none of the
TOOLS and none of the CUTTERS and NUTHIN' that we need to do our jobs!
They be talkin' about this TEAM thing – yeah, they want us to be on
THEIR team but are they on OURS?! Are they on OUR team when they lay us
off first chance they get?'

The manager chuckles condescendingly and says, 'Feel better, John?' Then
he narrows his eyes. 'Let's concentrate on something we can control!'

Like
giving everything we have to Goodstone Aircraft Company.

Custom-Fitted

Machinists
discard as soon as they can those legal
snub-nosed 35-pounds-of-air-pressure air nozzles,
and take up those illegal
105 or 110-pounds-of-air-pressure smuggled-through-the-shop
air nozzles and fit them with 3-foot-long barrels
and stick their trigger handles down into the slot-like ways
at the edges of their machine tables
so that their barrels stick up in the air like rifles.
These air guns
can blow razor-sharp chips twenty feet through the air
or drive them into the flesh of the hands
or face,
and they can fire
missiles made out of cardboard tubing 50 feet
through the air THWACK
into the tin wall of the building or the back
of another machinist,
whereas all the legal airguns can do
is clean off machine tables.

Why have something merely functional
when you can have something illegal and dangerous
and fun?

Sociable

I was never able to really talk to my fellow machinists
in the Goodstone Aircraft Company machine shop.
I would notice groups of 3 or 4 or 5 machinists
gathered at various machines
shooting the shit a mile a minute for 10 or 15 minutes
every day
but whenever I tried to go over to a machinist's machine and talk to him
or a group of machinists the conversation always seemed to die
almost immediately.
I tried talking about work and I tried not talking about work.
I tried being humorous.
I tried talking about politics.
I tried complaining about work and Goodstone Aircraft Company.
Nothing worked.

Until I finally tried
badmouthing my fellow machinists.
Immediately eyes lit up
and lengthy enthusiastic conversations began
that lasted 10 or 15 minutes or virtually as long as I wanted,
all kinds of other machinists and even supervisors wandering over
to join in and skewer and ridicule and character-assassinate.

Being popular
just requires a little effort.

Showing Us What He Can Do

Asked to train a couple of us machinists
on the Computer Numerically Controlled Mill machine the expert
Computer Numerically Controlled Mill operator makes sure
to go over all of what we must know
about the control box panel by
diligently going over the patterns of buttons we must push
to perform all of the functions we may want to perform
with the machine
over and over as many times as we want,
each time
moving his finger all over the panel hitting buttons with years-of-expertise
lightning-fast accuracy as our eyes inevitably
bug out and glaze over and our minds go blank
unable to absorb more than 10 or 20% of what he is doing.

After all,
one of a machinist's paramount skills is the ability
to keep secret and unavailable
as much of his skill
as possible.

Miscalculation

At the supervisor's daily talk
to us machinists in front of his machine shop bullpen the supervisor
is congratulating us
on having raised our production rate from 17%
to 21%
on our way to our goal of 24%,
and then
tells us that the Production Manager has decided
that there is no reason why we can't reach
40% production.

Wrong.
Not only does the inadequate tooling
and fucked up programming for our Computer Numerically Controlled machines
prohibit the likelihood of 40% production,
the fact that we machinists know
that a lot of us might very well be laid off
if we ever did attain 40% production,
makes it impossible.

Down to a Science

On the manufacturing orders to our jobs is given
the time
in decimal-form down to a thousandth of an hour that we should take to
make each part,
time figured out
by someone in an office somewhere and almost always
a million miles away from the actual time it takes to make the part,
and even though
we machinists and our Lead Men and our supervisors
have discussed with each other
over and over the lack of correspondence of these times
to reality,
we are still
held to them as our production rate is graphed and charted based on these times
and announced to us each week at Floor Action Meetings,
and we are still
given those cards with tables on them converting
the decimal times given on the manufacturing orders
to minutes and hours
so that we may better understand and follow them,
and we are still
given production level figures based on those times
such as 20% or 22% production
that we must reach
or face layoff.

No one up there in the offices ever seems to consider
trying to make the times given
more accurate.

Why should they tamper with a system
that works so well
already?

Make-Believe

Whenever they can machinists
like to pick up 6-inch-or-so-long and 1-inch-or-so-in-diameter
aluminum or steel aircraft
parts and hold them between their fingers like cigars
and lift them to their mouths and pretend to puff on them
with big Arnold Schwartzenegger grins or
stuff
those curved-barreled titanium parts that look like old
long-barreled revolvers
between their belts and pants on each hip and walk around
the shop swaggering and reaching for them like
they are walking down Wild West main streets toward gunfights.
They like to pick up those 4-foot-long aluminum tubes
and walk over to the machines of their favorite buddy machinists
and blow into the tubes as if they were trumpets while making imitation
trumpet sounds through their noses,
following this by announcing their buddies' names loudly and majestically
as if they were kings in their courts,
and they like to pick up those long hollow saxophone-like parts
to blow through them while dancing around their machines
and actually making some honking jazz-like
sounds.

Not everyone can turn their work area into a place
that's as much fun as their own backyard
when they were 6.

Getting Some Action

As the contract negotiations
between Goodstone Aircraft Company and the union neared their time limit Jack
at his machine threw his arms out.
'You know the union and the company's down in some resort hotel in Palm
Springs, don't ya? The whole thing's just a big show with a foregone
conclusion, and they get to have it done in PALM SPRINGS with SWIMMING
POOLS and GOLF COURSES and FANCY RESTAURANTS and SPAS and
       CALL GIRLS!'
he yelled
in protest at us machinists standing around him.
'They OUGHT to be having it out in a SWAMP somewhere where they could
hold each other by the leg out over some BIG ALLIGATORS and threaten to
let each other go!'

Now that's the kind of negotiating
machinists
could respect.

Getting Along

In the machine shop Ed had been taunting me
about being a nice guy,
leaving my machine a mess whenever he worked on it and
stealing jobs off of my machine whenever he could get away with it,
taunting me
because I never spoke meanly about anyone,
looking and peering and squinting at me
with eyes full of disgusted disbelief and derision
and hostility.
Until one day
when he came up to me at my machine I planted my feet
and stuck my face in his and screamed, 'Fuck you ED! Get the FUCK away
from me you SCUMBAG! You asshole! Fuck you you motherfucking ASSHOLE!'

For the first time
he looked and smiled at me
with real affection and respect.

Antiques

The old
manual machines sit
in the back of the machine shop older
than WW2 as old operators
retire that after 30 or 40 years on those machines
could do anything with them.
The machines sit
leaking oil and hydraulic fluid and operated
by men
who are nearing retirement or don't want to learn
the Computer Numerically Controlled machines
or can't learn them or
are crazy loners who like to hide off in the shadows
in the corners of the shop on those manual machines,
or by that one
maverick biker machinist down in the corner on the
1935 Bridgeport mill who
likes to beam with an ear to ear grin in the face of the Computer
Numerically Controlled operators
and raise his fist in the air in front of his face
and shake it
and shout, 'We're the last of the proud line of manual machine
operators!' like
it was better
than a Congressional Medal of Honor.

Eyes Open

Rick
takes a brush off the machine table and plunges it
into the big steel barrel full of pink oily coolant,
the coolant that sprays in a mist out of nozzles on our machines
onto parts we are making to keep them cool,
the coolant that fills the air around our machines
and that we daily
suck deep into our lungs.
He waves the brush around in the coolant and then yanks it
out dripping
with coolant and shouts, 'Hey Fred! This stuff really cleans great! Look!' and
slaps the brush up against the green side of the machine
that is covered with grease and grime and tiny metal chips
and brushes the coolant 4 or 5 times back and forth
across the side of the machine where it immediately
eats through all the grease and grime and chips and maybe a little
of the green paint as all of the filth
pours down with the coolant away from a now
perfectly clean spot
on the machine.
'Nope! This stuff won't hurt you a bit! It eats right through anything
you put it on but it's NOT HARMFUL TO US AT ALL!' Rick screams out
maniacally with the brush in his hand dripping coolant onto the concrete
floor. 'NEITHER WAS AGENT ORANGE!'

It's hard
to fool a veteran.

The $1 Solution

Everything
in the complex programming written in the programming
offices with the new million dollar
graphic programming machine to make the aircraft part
was perfect and everything
in the machinist's setting up of his machine's
elaborate computer controls
and axes locations and cutter computer offsets to make the part
was perfect and the first part
the machinist had cut on the super hot NEEDED-THIS-YESTERDAY job order
was perfect in all of its complex coordinate dimensions and compound
angles except
for that one $3/4$-degree angle
on the 3-inch-tall standing leg in the middle of the part
that programming had forgotten about,
and the supervisor and the Programming Liaison Man and the machine
operator were all extremely concerned and frustrated
about how long it would take to correct the complex program
until
the Lead Man came along and stuck the part into a vise
and picked up a hammer
and struck the thin standing leg of the part
with the hammer until it was on a roughly $3/4$-degree
angle.

In a pinch,
the human touch can still come in
mighty handy.

Ciphers

Veteran machinists at Goodstone Aircraft Company
look out of the corners of their eyes
and stick jaws out
and stroke handlebar moustaches and twinkle and untwinkle their eyes
and put half-smiles on their faces
that are impossible to read
as they talk and listen to each other on the shop floor.
Maybe they are laughing at each other.
Maybe they are laughing with each other.
Maybe they are angry.
Maybe they are sympathetic.
Maybe they are vulnerable.
Maybe they don't give a shit.
Maybe they are ready to kick each other's asses,
as their eyes dart about
and their smiles twitch on and off,
giving absolutely nothing away.

When you've worked 10 or 20 or 30 years
next to men
getting personal
interrogating you and taunting you and trying to crack you,
there's nothing more valuable
than the best poker face in the world.

Almost a Party Instead of a Job

Because every one of us with a job in the Goodstone Aircraft Company
machine shop had been laid off from Goodstone
at least once and in many cases
half a dozen or more times,
we whistled and sang as we worked,
we danced around our machines and laughed
constantly as the steel bins filled up with piles of aluminum chips
we made cutting slabs and blocks into aircraft parts.
We never talked or thought about tomorrow,
just about our next paychecks
and cases of expensive beer
and making wild love to our wives
and all the great places we could take them for dinner
and all the beautiful clothes we could buy them
and all the trips to Vegas we could take,
as the adrenalin rush
of being aircraft workers who were bound to get laid off again
but for now had a good paying job
pumped through our veins and we
drove to work in new cars and new shirts
and new shoes,
riding the crazy flights of our $22-an-hour aerospace jobs
before they crashed again.

Shifting Lives

Goodstone Aircraft Company machinists on first shift
work 7:08 am to 3:38 pm.
They exalt in being able to see their wives and families
and friends and prime time TV shows in the evenings
like normal people and they all dread
being forced by layoffs to go onto third shift
where machinists work 12:08 a.m. to 7:08 a.m.
and never get any REM sleep
and stand at their machines in a daze
or on speed
at the edge of nervous breakdown or illness
as they are forced to sleep in sealed-off air conditioned rooms
in the middle of the day,
or even worse
onto second shift where machinists
work 3:38 pm to 12:08 am
and never
get to see their wives or families or friends or prime time TV shows
except on weekends
as their marriages weaken or fall apart and they begin to feel
like people from another planet.

Though they all agree
none of these is nearly as bad as fourth shift,
that one a machinist does
out on the sidewalks
after he's laid off.

Paradise

In the 1970s when I was young
the factories each had their flavor as I drove up to them
looking for work.
There were the little tin ones
on gravel with a row of Hell's Angel-type motorcycles in front of them
and the smell of County Jail and toxic chemicals that I drove by
slowly 2 or 3 times with a half-sick stomach
trying to decide whether or not to go in even though I knew
I'd probably be hired.
There were big factories
with proud signs sporting company logos atop their roofs
on endless asphalt under blazing suns that roared
with blast furnaces and 10-ton machines that I knew
were Hells on earth and there
were the little 1-man machine shops like dental offices with the owners
that would squeeze as many keys or tubes or drill casings
or slotted steel shafts or hex nuts as possible
out of me for every penny of the low wage they paid me
and there
were all those huge aerospace companies with endless buildings
on vast lots
that would swallow me up with good pay and then spit me out
in savings-account-draining layoffs until I'd hung on working there long
enough that I wasn't fit to work anywhere else
and could never leave.

Never again would there be so many poisons
to pick from.

Not Gone Yet

They disappear
from the machine shop,
bikers
with their toolboxes sitting on their workbenches locked
for weeks
until they reappear with their jaws wired shut
or metal plates in their skulls to tell us
about their latest crashes,
mental cases
gone for weeks until their wives finally find them
sitting on park benches or beaches
staring up at the sky with their mouths dropped open,
insanely jealous
machinists absent from their machines until
they finish serving jail sentences for going berserk
with baseball bats.
They all
put their hands around the handles of their machines again
and smile,
glad
and grateful that they have been saved,
glad
that they aren't among those we never see again,
those who disappear for good
in Mexico
or during the 1992 L.A. riots
or into the ground
after final drink and drug binges,
so glad
that they still have these machine handles
to hang onto.

Something Only the Decades Can Teach

Now at 46
I am becoming the machine shop veteran I once stared at in amazement
when I was 22.
Now I am becoming
the character with the gnarled fingers
and the crazy eyes
and the teller of the jokes and the tales that come spewing out of
my mouth
before I even know it.
Now I know
what 25 or 45 years on grinding wheels
or saws or the floorboards in front of horizontal milling machines
with arbors turning 100 pounds of gang mills
can do to a man,
what the foreman
and the owners and the streets of laid-off desperation
can do,
as a life
spent between the tin walls of shops
begins to close in on me
and I know I will never escape.
Now I know it in my bones
and in my dreams at night
and in each and every line on my face
and laugh or tear in my heart
as I wish
so very much that I could make just one of those 22-year-old new-hires
staring at me in such amazed curiosity
understand.

AMERICAN POETRY
FROM BLOODAXE BOOKS

for a complete catalogue, please write to:
Bloodaxe Books Ltd, P.O. Box 1SN, Newcastle upon Tyne NE99 1SN.